THE LIBRARY OF ENGL

GENERAL EDITOR: C. M. W

ENGLISH WATER-COLOURS

THE LIBRARY OF ENGLISH ART

ENGLISH WATER-COLOURS
LAURENCE BINYON, C.H.
Sometime Keeper of Prints and Drawings, British Museum

ENGLISH POTTERY AND PORCELAIN
W. B. HONEY
Sometime Keeper of the Department of Ceramics, Victoria & Albert Museum
Fifth edition, revised by R. J. Charleston

ENGLISH NEEDLEWORK
A. F. KENDRICK
Sometime Keeper of the Department of Textiles, Victoria & Albert Museum

ENGLISH DOMESTIC SILVER
CHARLES OMAN
Keeper of the Department of Metalwork, Victoria & Albert Museum

ENGLISH FURNITURE
JOHN GLOAG
Author of 'The English Tradition in Design', 'Georgian Grace', etc.

ENGLISH GLASS
W. A. THORPE
Author of 'A History of English and Irish Glass', etc.
Sometime Deputy Keeper in the Victoria & Albert Museum

THE ENGLISH PRINT
BASIL GRAY
Keeper in the British Museum

ENGLISH PORTRAIT MINIATURES
GRAHAM REYNOLDS
Keeper in the Victoria & Albert Museum

FRANCIS TOWNE.   THE SOURCE OF THE ARVEIRON

ENGLISH
WATER-COLOURS

BY

LAURENCE BINYON, C.H.
LATELY KEEPER OF PRINTS AND DRAWINGS
BRITISH MUSEUM

SECOND EDITION
With a frontispiece in colour
and thirty-two plates in photogravure

ADAM & CHARLES BLACK
LONDON

FIRST EDITION 1933
SECOND EDITION 1944
REPRINTED 1946
REPRINTED 1962

C 20185375.

PRINTED IN GREAT BRITAIN
BY R. & R. CLARK LTD, EDINBURGH

TO
C. J. HOLMES
**IN FRIENDSHIP AND
IN MEMORY OF YOUTH**

PREFACE
TO THE SECOND EDITION

THIS edition is reprinted from the first with a few small corrections and additions which Laurence Binyon had noted in his own copy. When the publisher told him that a new edition was contemplated he wrote that on looking through the book again he did not feel that any extensive alterations were called for, but that he would perhaps say a little more about contemporary artists. This he did not live to do. But when the publisher suggested the addition of eight illustrations to the twenty-five in the first edition, it seemed an opportunity to fall in with his intention by choosing half of these to represent the work of four contemporary artists. Brief biographical notes on them have been added at the end of Chapter XIII.

BASIL GRAY

PREFACE
TO THE FIRST EDITION

HAVING, long ago, spent ten years of my life in cataloguing the English Drawings in the British Museum, I have retained an affectionate interest in the subject, especially in the work of certain artists. In writing this little book, however, I have been greatly indebted to the labours of others. All those who are interested in English Water-colours know how much has been done in late years for the study of the chief masters, and the rescue from oblivion of minor but not negligible artists, by a group of scholars and enthusiasts: Mr. C. F. Bell, Mr. A. P. Oppé, Mr. Finberg, Mr. Randall Davies, Mr. Girtin, Mr. A. G. B. Russell, Mr. Isherwood Kay, Mr. Kitson, Mr. C. E. Hughes—these and others by their researches have added greatly to our store of accurate and detailed information; and a special acknowledgment is owing to the Walpole Society, founded in 1911, because it has provided a means of publication for so much of this work, which might otherwise have languished in manuscript or never been undertaken. All this fresh material, together with new facts and records appearing for the first

time in Farington's Diaries, was due to be collected
and incorporated in a book intended for the general
reader; and at the same time a revaluation of the
achievements of the school might well be thought
desirable.

I am indebted to Mr. C. F. Bell, Mr. Kitson, Mr.
Girtin, and Mrs. Esdaile, for information privately
communicated.

I wish to thank all those by whose labours I
have profited, and not less those owners and authori-
ties of museums and public galleries who have
courteously allowed me to enrich these pages with
reproductions of drawings in their possession.

L. B.

CONTENTS

CONTENTS

LIST OF PLATES

ILLUSTRATIONS

ENGLISH WATER-COLOURS

THE FORERUNNERS

ON the 9th of April 1585 a little fleet of seven ships sailed from Plymouth into the Atlantic. They were fitted out by Sir Walter Raleigh, whose high hope was to found the first English colony in North America. Among the adventurers on board was John White, a man of middle age, experienced in travel. He carried with him a box of colours; for he combined with other functions that of draughtsman to the expedition. And in Virginia—really North Carolina, but 'Virginia' had not yet a defined frontier and covered a vague stretch of coast—John White made a number of drawings in water-colour.

In 1590 appeared at Frankfort-am-Main the first volume of Theodore de Bry's great work *America*. De Bry had come to London in 1588 and made the acquaintance of Richard Hakluyt; who introduced him to John White. From White's drawings he chose twenty-three which he had engraved for the reprint of Hariot's Report on Virginia which was incorporated in *America*. These engravings have served at second, third, and fourth hand as material for all

book-illustrations of the natives of Virginia ever
since. The drawings from which they were made
were lost from sight, and no one supposed that they
survived.

But in 1865 a book of drawings from an old
library in Ireland appeared in a sale at Sotheby's.
They were recognised as White's lost drawings by
that enthusiastic student of American discovery,
Henry Stevens of Vermont; he bought the volume,
and from him it was purchased for the British
Museum.

English water-colours are usually thought to begin
with the 'stained' drawings on an Indian-ink foundation of the eighteenth century. But let us claim for
them a more gallant beginning, in the days of
Elizabeth, when Michael Drayton was writing his
stanzas *To the Virginian Voyage*, flushed with eager
expectation of rediscovering the Golden Age on
those shores, where the vines came down to the sea
'so that the spray beat over them'. Did not Sir
Richard Grenville of the *Revenge* sail with John
White as 'General'? In fact we see him in one of these
drawings riding at the head of a troop in an island
of the West Indies, just as is described in Hakluyt's
pages. There follow pictures of the Indians in their
various occupations, and single figures, and birds,
and plants, and fishes. Other drawings, not made in
Virginia, but in Florida, Greenland, and remote

parts of Europe, are included in the book, and testify to White's wide experience of travel.

These drawings show little restriction in the range of colour, which is applied directly with no grey under-painting. The pigments are of course not so finely ground, and the washes therefore less transparent, than in the later art. John White was not drawing with an artistic purpose, but to record and give information; but his method and use of his materials are much the same as Dürer's in his water-colour landscapes. And though he would not have claimed to be more than a 'draughtsman', he wins our interest, not only for his association with the romance of Raleigh's ill-fated 'First Colonie', which disappeared and took no lasting hold, but because, though there must have been other Englishmen doing the same kind of work at that time, his name has survived, and we can attach it with certainty to actual drawings which have a genuine merit, a sensitive quality, of their own.

Artists of native birth were not numerous in England in the sixteenth century. The water-colour medium was chiefly used by the 'limners' or portrait-painters in miniature, of whom that exquisite 'Little Master', Nicholas Hilliard, was the chief. To treat of the English miniature-painters would enlarge the scope of this volume too much. Still less is there room for dealing with the illuminators of the medieval

2

manuscripts; each of these large groups of artists demands a separate book, though in both cases the medium was water-colours.

The days of the illuminated manuscripts were over; the Reformation and the fanaticism of Puritan iconoclasts had utterly broken the continuity of tradition in English art; only the crafts survived; and limning, now that painting had lost the patronage of the Church, was almost the only sort of pictorial art to be practised.

John White was not a professional painter, but he had obviously received a training from some professional artists. Henry Stevens conjectured that he was a pupil of Jacques Le Moyne, the French painter who accompanied Laudonnière's expedition to Florida in 1564–65; but such work of Le Moyne's as I have seen bears no similarity to White's work. It was rather from an artist of the Low Countries that he seems to have learnt, as some fanciful drawings by him of Ancient Britons betray. These have the flamboyant mannerisms of Italianised Flemings and Dutchmen. And this is what we should expect, for it was with the art of the Low Countries that English art was then most in contact.

Dürer's landscape drawings are the first notable water-colour landscapes in Europe. There are many of these in the museums of Europe, including the British Museum.

4

But apart from Dürer the water-colour medium was used in Europe by artists quite sporadically; there was no established tradition. Holbein's designs for jewels, Giovanni da Udine's decorations, are exceptional. Later, in the seventeenth century, we have the charming water-colours of Adrian van Ostade.

The medium was, however, much used by draughtsmen of various nationalities, who, like White, were also travellers, or illustrators of natural history.

In England, water-colours began to be used in the seventeenth century not only for small portraits, but for figure-subjects—what used to be called 'history'[1] —and for landscapes. About 1630 or a little earlier Edward Norgate wrote a treatise, *Miniatura, or the Art of Limning*, for Sir Theodore Mayerne. It was much copied and pirated, and twenty years later, a little before his death in 1650, he revised and enlarged it. The revision introduces for the first time a section on landscape. This second edition of *Miniatura* has been reprinted by Mr. Martin Hardie, and it shows that water-colour landscapes were being painted in England, though 'an Art soe new in England' that the name had to be borrowed from

[1] Isaac Oliver (*d.* 1617) in his will bequeathed 'his drawings . . . and Limning pictures, be they historyes, stories,' etc. His *Entombment* was much admired. This was left unfinished and completed by Isaac's son Peter, noted for his water-colour copies of oil-pictures.

the Dutch. 'To say truth the Art is theirs, and the best in that kind that ever I saw speake Dutch, viz., Paulo Brill . . . and his contemporary Adam Elshamer . . . Momper, Brueghel, Coningslo, and last but not least, Sr Peter Rubens.'

Beautiful examples of Rubens' landscape drawings, both in transparent and opaque colours, are in the Print Room. There also are landscapes by Van Dyck, in both styles. And two delightful drawings in body-colours on bluish paper (three, if we add another recently acquired example, to which an obscure artist's name has been wrongly, as I think, attached) have all the look of drawings made in England. There is a drawing of Rye in the Pierpont Morgan Collection, but this is in pen-and-ink.

These Van Dyck drawings already anticipate the landscape drawings of Gainsborough in their breadth and fluent grace. But till we come to Gainsborough, there is no evidence that the landscape style of Rubens and Van Dyck was followed in England. Probably such landscapes as must have been painted, since Norgate writes of the art being practised here, were in the smaller manner of painters like Paul Brill. The inspiration of Italian art possessed only Inigo Jones, through whom more than anyone else the Italian Renaissance affected art in England. In the famous sketch-book at Chatsworth, published as

6

the Walpole Society's twelfth volume, water-colour is used in some of the designs for dresses, but the drawings for scenery are in sepia wash or pen-and-ink. What English artists practised the newly introduced art of landscape we do not know, nor can we point to their works; yet it is likely enough that some work of theirs survives, nameless, in old country houses, probably done in opaque colours.

English water-colour art, however, was not to develop from these traditions. A new beginning was to be made. It is true that there is a continuity in one kind of water-colour from Elizabeth's time onwards, and that is in the tradition of the small portrait. But the English miniature is, as I have said, a subject for separate treatment which cannot be attempted here. Wenzel Hollar (1607–77) came to England in 1635. We owe a debt of gratitude to this indefatigable Bohemian, for through him better than anyone else we can picture how ordinary folk, not the great ladies and gentlemen of Van Dyck, appeared on their walks abroad; we know the streets and alleys of the London of that time, the life of Thames-side, the rural uplands and villages long since covered by houses and pavements. And not London alone, but many another part of England. Hollar's drawings were mostly intended to be etched; they are essentially pen-drawings, but often washed with water-colour. *The Tower from the Thames* in the Print Room is a pleasant example. The tints of grey and blue are foiled by the pink of bricks and tiles; it is the pale sunshine of the North; there is a breeze stirring, one can hear the ripple of water against the ship anchored opposite the Tower. More elaborate, and with more colour, is the series of drawings of Tangier, some of large size, whither Hollar was sent as draughtsman in 1689.

Hollar had an English friend at York, Francis Place, who though not a professional artist made a number of drawings in this modest but attractive style, and also etched. Francis Place was not actually a pupil of Hollar's—he lamented that he had not been—but was intimately acquainted with him and followed his manner in drawing and etching. He had means of his own, but his chief preoccupation, apart from sport (and he was a great fisherman in his youth), was with the arts. He experimented with the manufacture of porcelain, but did not persevere; he was impatient of task-work and liked to follow his fancy. He worked chiefly in the North of England, but also in London. Born in 1647, he died in 1728. The series of letters published, with a catalogue of Place's etchings and mezzotints, by Mr. H. M. Hake in the Walpole Society's publications (vol. x., 1922), gives us a glimpse into a pleasant circle of artists and art-lovers in a period when English art is often supposed to have been non-existent; of Place, his great friend

Henry Gyles, the glass-painter of York, Francis Barlow, William Lodge, John Lambert, and Ralph Thoresby. Barlow was a good painter of sporting subjects and is remembered also for his illustrations to Æsop's fables; he drew in Indian-ink and in sepia, and very likely in water-colour also.

The forty-odd drawings by Place in the British Museum are mostly views in his native Yorkshire, especially of York itself. Old buildings and ruins interested him, but he also liked prospects of sea and coast. Some of these drawings are very pleasing, without being remarkable. A drawing of Knaresborough recalls some of the Dutch masters. In some sketches of ducks more colour is used than in the landscapes. At South Kensington there is a charming drawing tinted with colour, of Thames-side at Millbank looking towards Westminster and London.

It is possible to trace a continuous thread of tradition in the water-colour school, a tradition of landscape based on topography, from Hollar and Place through Samuel Scott and the Sandbys, Rooker, Hearne, and Dayes, to Girtin and Turner.

It is quite true that this is the only continuity we can find in the school apart, as I have said, from the limners and miniaturists; and perhaps it was natural that nineteenth-century writers who conceived of water-colour art as purely a British art should have propagated the notion of a gradual advance from the stained drawings of views by the Sandby school to the transformation effected by Girtin and Turner, the change from water-colour drawing to water-colour painting. It seemed a neat and orderly progress. But for one thing this theory ignores the figure-painters, so that people have become accustomed to associate our water-colour school entirely with landscape; and for another thing it doesn't square with the facts.

Let us discard for a moment our tendency to magnify movements and developments and look at the artists themselves. If we cast a glance over the chief practitioners in the water-colour medium during the eighteenth century, who are the artists who really count? It is Gainsborough, Alexander and John Cozens, Sandby, Rowlandson, Francis Towne, and Blake. At the very close of the century there are splendid drawings by Girtin and Turner; but these two masters are not only the continuators and transformers of the native topographical tradition, they have other predecessors and are much affected by the art of the Continent.

There is no neat and orderly progress, apart from the line of the topographers, to use a term which is convenient, though more depreciatory than is just. Instead, we have an array of very diverse and individual artists.

There is another point. The conception of a technical advance from drawing to painting, and especially of an advance from reticent tinting over a monochrome foundation to direct painting in colour, is only true if we confine our attention to the 'topographers'. Already early in the century we find drawings by Taverner, and a little later by Skelton, in which there is variety of colour and no grey underpainting; so with George Robertson, with Pars, with Towne, and amateurs like Gore and Reveley. These men often used a fuller range of colour than Girtin ever did. The earlier of these artists, Taverner and Skelton, and to them we must add Paul Sandby, sometimes painted in body-colours, or in transparent and opaque colour at once. And it is significant that in all these cases there is influence from Continental practice. Low tones were the rule in the oil painting of the period, and water-colours were naturally affected by that example.

In the sixteenth and seventeenth centuries English art was in contact with the art of the Netherlands more than with any other tradition of the Continent. But by the eighteenth century the great age of Dutch as of Flemish painting was past; and it was Rome which drew the thoughts of aspiring artists. In the domain of landscape it was not actually Italian masters who had the great prestige, it was the two French masters working in Rome, Claude Lorrain and Gaspar Poussin, though Salvator Rosa no doubt attracted certain temperaments. Later in the century there is, as Mr. Bell has shown, considerable emulation with the Swiss school of water-colour painters, notably Ducros.

EARLY EIGHTEENTH CENTURY PAINTERS

THERE is a little painting in water-colours and body-colours in the British Museum which, from the costumes represented, must date from the first years of the eighteenth century, though a false earlier date has been added to it. It is anonymous and represents a coffee-house. Men are seated at narrow tables reading the news-sheets, while a boy pours out their coffee; one is standing up with a candle to have a better look at a landscape on the wall. Four pots of coffee stand before a blazing fire, and a woman behind a canopied desk dispenses 'Irish Usquebaugh' to another young waiter. It is an interesting document of the period rather than a work of art; but it shows the kind of work practised at that time. Probably it is by a foreign hand. Another drawing, also in water-colour and body-colour, in the same collection, is of historical interest, since it represents Sir Robert Walpole haranguing his Cabinet, and is remarkable for its varied and bright colouring. Obviously the notion that the landscape draughtsmen used such limited colours because more were

not available is absurd. This drawing is by 'Goupy';
but I am not certain whether it is by Louis Goupy,
who died in 1747, or his nephew Joseph, who was
made cabinet-painter to Frederick Prince of Wales
in 1732. Joseph Goupy painted scenes for the opera
in conjunction with Peter Tillemans, whose gouache
drawings of country scenes, hunting and riding, are
well known. There is a small landscape by Joseph
Goupy in the Print Room, very much derived from
Salvator, rich in colour. He also made water-colour
copies of Raphael's Cartoons.

Another artist who painted theatre-scenery was
Zuccarelli, who came to England through John
Smith, the British Consul at Venice, who also
brought over Canaletto. Zuccarelli, after an interval
in Italy, returned to England in 1752 and stayed
twenty years, becoming one of the foundation
members of the Royal Academy. His landscapes in
body-colour with gaily-dressed pastoral figures were
pretty and very popular, though his drawings in pen
and bistre are much better.

These artists were all foreign-born, and it is characteristic of them that they were painters rather than
draughtsmen and used body-colour freely. That,
rather than transparent colour, was the Continental
mode. But it did not so much appeal to the English;
though, as we shall see, certain artists, who had con-
tacts with Italy or with Italian art, used body-colours

as well as transparent colours, often on the same drawing.

In landscape the opaque pigment was felt perhaps to be unsuitable for the rendering of English atmosphere. There is in the Print Room a little painting in body-colour by John Laporte, the teacher of Dr. Monro; it is a view of Grasmere, but is made to look like an Italian lake. But even in figure-subjects the Englishmen preferred transparent washes, giving emphasis and energy to the contours with a pen.

In the early part of the eighteenth century English artists were little in favour; foreigners had all the vogue. But Hogarth was gradually asserting himself, and the tide began to turn.

On a May morning in 1732 Hogarth with a party of four friends started for a five days' tour in the Island of Sheppey. The friends were Tothall, Samuel Scott, Thornhill, Hogarth's father-in-law, and Ebenezer Forrest. The 'peregrination' was recorded in a little account written by Forrest and illustrated with seven drawings by Hogarth and two by Scott. The book is now in the British Museum; it was published with aquatints by R. Livesay in 1782. The drawings are in pen-and-wash, with a little colour. The best of them is a scene in the inn at Stoke, where a fisherman is shaving Thornhill, Tothall is shaving himself, Forrest is breakfasting, Scott and Hogarth drawing, quill in hand. As often with Hogarth, the pen-line, considered by itself, has a loose, rather wavering look, yet somehow an astonishing sense of living people is conveyed. Here, as still more in a large Conversation Piece of ladies and gentlemen on a terrace, also in the Print Room, though little colour is used, it is used to very happy effect. But more often, as in the series of Industry and Idleness, Hogarth was content with Indian-ink alone; and oils were more congenial to his brush.

Samuel Scott was also an oil painter, but painted frequently in water-colours. Born about 1710,[1] he died in 1772. He had a place in the Stamp Office, took up painting as an amusement and made of it a profitable profession. He lived in Covent Garden, retired to Ludlow, then to Bath, where he died. He painted London scenes, especially of Thames-side. Though called a marine painter he was never at sea but once, when he went in a yacht sent to Helvoetsluys to bring over George II. Edward Dayes said of Scott that 'he was the first to make his drawings approach the strength of oil pictures'. This is a surprising assertion, for the known water-colours by him are more timid than vigorous, though he shows a genuine feeling for the beauty of old brick-work and gliding water; and, as we have seen, contemporaries were using a full range of colour, at any rate in the opaque

[1] According to Farington, quoting Marlow, he died in 1772 at the age of seventy.

method. Scott's one landscape in the 'Tour' is scarcely coloured at all.

Ebenezer Forrest, who wrote the account of the 'Tour', has been confused by Redgrave with his son Theodosius (1728–84), by whom there is a water-colour of St. Botolph's Priory, Colchester, with figures, in the Print Room. It is somewhat in the style of Sandby, but more closely resembles certain drawings by J. Skelton, another contemporary. Very little is known of Skelton, but he is quite an interesting artist. We infer from his drawings that he worked at Rochester and Canterbury and in Surrey. He was also in Italy for a time, probably at the end of his life. There is a quiet beauty in his *Sandpit, Croydon*, and a luminous breadth in a *Scene on the Medway*, both in the Print Room, which betray a real sensibility. A *Tivoli* in the same collection is less successful. There is a Roman view at South Kensington; and there is a very good *Albano* in the Whitworth Institute, Manchester, strong in its effect. In these and other drawings the colouring is sober but there is little monochrome underpainting. Skelton died in 1758.

I may mention here a rather surprising drawing of a country-house seen from a distance, by Francis Cotes, which has recently been acquired by the Victoria and Albert Museum. It is signed and dated 1750. Cotes has hitherto been known for his able portraits, and for his pastels. There is a charming group by him in the Print Room in Indian-ink and colour, of Queen Charlotte with her baby and the Duchess of Ancaster, reproduced in colour by Mr. Davies in his *Social Life in the Eighteenth Century*. But that he should paint a landscape in water-colours with so much mastery of the medium is an unsuspected discovery. Admirers of Downman's charming little portraits may also, by the way, be surprised to know what a gift that painter had for landscape. A series of studies, lightly coloured, in Mr. Oppé's collection makes one wish that he had devoted more of his time to landscape-painting. One of them, a study of a tree-trunk with plants in the foreground, is a remarkable thing to find in the eighteenth century. But this is to anticipate: for Downman belongs to a later period, he was not born till 1750, the year of Cotes' water-colour.

Among Scott's pupils were William Marlow and Sawrey Gilpin. Gilpin, whose brother William was an amateur artist and wrote several treatises on the Picturesque, assisted Scott in some of his pictures; he painted animals, especially horses. There are tinted water-colours by him. But as a water-colour painter Marlow, though he also painted in oils, is more important. He studied under Scott for five years, from about 1756 (Farington's Diary). He was born in 1740. He worked in France and Italy, 1765–68, and painted Italian scenes, influenced by Richard Wilson, also English country-seats and views in London. Something of the Hogarthian tradition can be traced in his rather loose drawing; he is always more the painter than the draughtsman in his water-colours. He used a fairly full range of colour.

Contemporary with Scott, but standing rather aloof from his fellow-artists, was William Taverner. Born in 1703, the son of an inferior dramatist, he was procurator-general of the Court of Arches at Canterbury, but devoted his spare time to art. According to Sawrey Gilpin, as reported by Farington in the Diary, Taverner 'had much quaiking about showing his pictures; which raised their reputation'. He carried his coyness so far that Scott quarrelled with him because, after promising to do so, he refused to show his paintings to a friend of Scott's. He died in 1773.

Taverner's reputation, great in his own day, declined considerably when his work faced the daylight in the sale-room. The mythological or pastoral figures which he was fond of putting into his landscapes were feebly drawn. But his landscape drawings are pleasing enough. Probably he is seen at his best in a large drawing, or rather painting, in the British Museum of *Sand-pits at Woolwich*, with a cart coming along a sunken road. This is partly in body-colour, and is conceived very much as a Gaspar Poussin landscape, yet retains a flavour of English soil and English character. But in artistic feeling as in accomplishment Taverner is inferior to the almost unrecorded Skelton.

One other artist may conveniently be mentioned here, though actually he should come a little later in our story, since he was not born till 1747. This is George Robertson, who has been rescued from time's obscurity by Mr. C. F. Bell. He died in early middle age, in 1788. Robertson, again, is one of the artists who came under the Roman spell. He was taken to Italy by William Beckford the elder, and spent some time in Rome, working with Pannini and with Joseph Vernet. Afterwards he was taken by the same patron to Jamaica. Returning to England, he became a teacher. He was employed by Boydell to make some large drawings which Boydell had engraved and published. Among these is a set of drawings of Ironworks in Coalbrookdale, Shropshire; a rather surprising subject for the period; but the best known are two oval views of Windsor, one of which shows a Royal Party on the Terrace. In spite of these publications, Robertson is said to have had 'no very brilliant success with the publick'. He suffered from ill-health.

When in England, Robertson painted in transparent colours, but, like Taverner, mixed his methods and used body-colour in the nearer parts of his landscapes. No doubt he found that landscapes in the body-colour technique, as practised on the Continent,

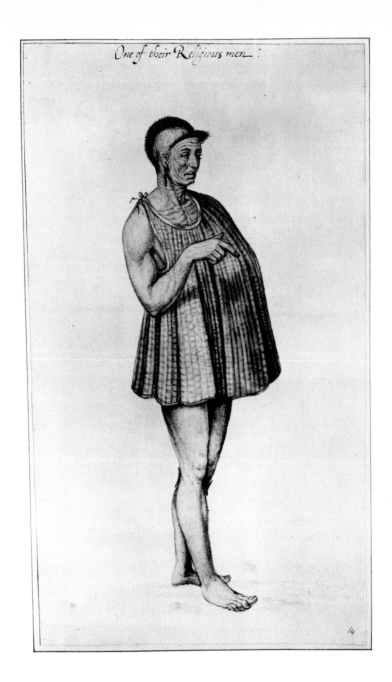

One of their Religious men :

JOHN WHITE. A PRIEST

PAUL SANDBY.   KITTY FISHER AS A MILKMAID

looked scenic and airless beside the luminous drawings made in the transparent method; but to redress
the weakness of the stained drawings he would en-
force the foliage of trees with opaque pigment. He
usually introduced figures into his landscapes, sometimes from Biblical or classic story, with a decided
reminiscence of Gaspar Poussin; these are less feeble
but more mannered than Taverner's; but he is happier
with real rustics, though these have a touch of slightly
unnatural elegance. Robertson is well represented in
the Ashmolean and in the British Museum. He is
an artist of some interest but rather isolated and
ineffectual. His work looks as if it belonged to an
earlier period than it actually does.

Two painters who were Robertson's contemporaries, in fact both of them older than he by a few
years, William Pars and Francis Towne, are of more
importance in our story: both worked on the Continent as well as in England, but kept an English
style. These men, however, group themselves rather
with J. R. Cozens and others of the 'Southern' school
(as one might call it); and it is time to return to the
topographers and to the man who in some ways must
be regarded as the central figure in English water-
colours of the eighteenth century, Paul Sandby.

III

PAUL SANDBY AND HIS FOLLOWERS

THE art of landscape-painting in China is said to have grown out of the art of map-making for military purposes. The landscapes of Thomas and Paul Sandby had a similar foundation; for these two brothers began as military draughtsmen. Thomas was twenty, Paul sixteen, when they left their native Nottingham for London in 1741, and worked for a time in the Survey Office in the Tower. Two years later Thomas became draughtsman to the Duke of Cumberland and made with him the campaigns of 1743 and 1745 on the Continent, and against the Young Pretender in England and Scotland. Like Hollar at Tangier, he drew camps and fortifications; some of these views are in the MSS. department of the British Museum.

Thomas Sandby became an architect. He was appointed Deputy Ranger of Windsor Forest, and was occupied for years in the construction of the Virginia Water. His drawings are similar in style to those of his brother, but more confined in range. They are also much rarer, for he has nothing of Paul's importance as a landscape draughtsman. Not that Paul Sandby was a landscape painter merely; he was also good at figures, drawing them with vivacity and grouping them with grace. After the '45 rebellion, a survey of the Highlands was undertaken by Government, and Paul Sandby was appointed draughtsman to the Survey. Between 1745 and 1751 he was thus employed. In the Print Room are sixty-eight sketches of scenes and groups of people made in Edinburgh and the neighbourhood; they show a keen eye for character and comedy. Men and women in argument; crowds at a fair; lookers-on at the execution of a rebel in the Grassmarket; two noted rebels in their plaids handcuffed between soldiers; a scene in the High Street; a game of chess; such are some of the subjects of these sketches, which vividly evoke the place and time.

Later, Sandby drew a set of London Street Cries, twelve of which were etched; and he attacked Hogarth in some caricatures. It is of course as a landscape painter that he is best known; but even these often owe much to the figures introduced. The *Drawwell, Broughton, near Edinburgh*, a drawing made in 1751, is a charming example of Sandby's simpler style. It is in the Print Room. The pink tiles of a roof pleasantly foil the cool greys and blues; but the tall figure of a girl in a straw hat advancing all in shadow against the sky is what makes the drawing

23

as design. 'Pleasant' is the word for the typical Sandby drawing of this kind. Such are the drawings of Windsor and of Eton, filled with cool sunshine, of which he made so many. We enjoy them because they do not attempt more than is within the artist's means, and they are very accomplished.

But Sandby used more than one style, and, in his later years especially, employed body-colours, sometimes on blue paper. Again he sometimes used body-colours and transparent colours together, with or without a reed-pen outline. He himself preferred his body-colour drawings, as having more of the character of painting; but few would now share in this opinion, for in this medium his draughtsmanship is inadequate, his touch less certain. He attempts by means of opaque colour to give massiveness to the great oaks in his woodland scenes; but he fails to seize the main lines of growth, and becomes confused in the foliage. He is far happier with his transparent technique and with trees of more feminine grace like the ash and the willow.

Some of his drawings in pen-and-wash are happy in their effect. They seem to show the influence of Gainsborough, and have been occasionally taken for the work of that master. Sandby was impressionable and lived to be eighty-four. He greatly admired and sometimes copied Richard Wilson, whose drawings he bought when that artist was very poor. One or two of his late drawings may perhaps owe something to Girtin, who came to be his neighbour in 1800 in St. George's Row, Tyburn, where Sandby had bought a house in 1772. There are many water-colours by him of this Bayswater neighbourhood, then on the outskirts of London. From here Sandby would drive to Woolwich, where he was drawing-master from 1768 to 1796, not without fear of high-waymen on Blackheath.

Among the multitude of Sandby drawings there is much that is delightful, if there are no masterpieces. As a landscape painter he had no passion. He is at his best perhaps in the series of Encampments in around London in 1780, at the time of Lord George Gordon's agitation and the No Popery Riots, engraved in aquatint by the artist. Two of these are in the British Museum. But of all his drawings I think the most charming is a portrait of Kitty Fisher, freely drawn with a brush in water-colours, which is at Windsor. It is reproduced here, facing page 21.

Limited in gift as he is, in spite of his variety, Paul Sandby is of real importance in the water-colour school. He was productive over a long period of years. More than any other artist, it was he who re-vealed to English people the beauty of their own country. He travelled all over England and Wales, also in Scotland and Ireland, and his drawings be-came widely known through the aquatints he engraved from them: it was a process which he introduced into England. His art was thoroughly English in character. He was followed by a number of painters who worked in the same tradition.

John Cleveley (*b.* 1747, *d.* 1786) was the son of a Deptford shipwright, and making acquaintance with Paul Sandby, then teaching at Woolwich, he learnt the art of water-colours from him. Later he painted also in oils, but had less ease in that medium. He made a name by his river-side scenes, drawings of docks and shipping, and in 1772 was chosen to be draughtsman to Sir Joseph Banks on his voyage to the Orkneys and Iceland. In 1773 he went with Captain Phipps' expedition to the North Seas, and two water-colours made on the voyage are in the Print Room.

John Cleveley's twin brother Robert also painted in water-colours but is better known by his oil pictures of naval actions, which were numerous and much admired. He died in 1809. Another marine painter of the period was Nicholas Pocock (*b.* about 1741, *d.* 1821). If the shipping in the Thames inspired the Cleveleys, Pocock owed a similar debt to his native Bristol. He was in fact a sailor himself before he adopted art as a profession; sailed to South Carolina and the West Indies, and made numerous sketches afterwards used in finished works. Pocock made a great reputation by his sea pieces and naval battles, but he also made water-colours of landscape, sometimes with rustic figures. In his late years he became one of the foundation members of the Water-Colour Society. His drawings are pleasing in their modest way.

Two popular painters and drawing-masters may conveniently be mentioned here: Francis Nicholson and William Payne. Nicholson came from Yorkshire, Payne from Devonshire, but both worked also in London. Nicholson was noted for the introduction in his landscapes of the device of stopping out the lights, which Turner sometimes employed. He was born in 1753 and died in 1844. He was a mannered artist. Payne also was a mannerist, but a more interesting painter. He was a most successful teacher in his day.

Among the direct followers of Paul Sandby the most notable men are M. A. Rooker (1743–1801) and Thomas Hearne (1744–1817). Rooker was actually a pupil of Sandby, in painting; in engraving, which he also practised, he was trained by his father. He was elected A.R.A. in 1770. The *Copper-Plate Magazine* (1775–77), which did so much to popularise the Views of country houses and picturesque spots in Britain, contains a great amount of his work. He was scene-painter to the Haymarket Theatre (where he was known as 'Rooker-ini'); but he is now remembered by his water-colour drawings of landscapes and buildings. These have an attractive dainty neatness and pleasing quiet colour.

Hearne's drawings have the same sober merits, though his colouring is apt to be dull. He began as an engraver, being apprenticed to Woollett, with whom he stayed six years. In 1771 he went to the Leeward Islands with the newly appointed governor and worked there for over three years. In 1777 he began, with William Byrne, the main work of his life, the *Antiquities of Great Britain*. He made fifty-two drawings for the book, which occupied him till 1781. Hearne was indeed as much antiquary as artist.

Thomas Malton belonged to the same generation. Born in 1748, he was the son of an architectural draughtsman of the same name; he made numbers of drawings of London, well known through aquatints, neat and sober but prosaic.

Edward Dayes (1763–1804), in the next generation, was a more ambitious artist. He, too, is now known mainly by his 'views' in water-colour; but, like Sandby, he drew figures admirably, and one of his finest drawings, the *Buckingham House, St. James's Park* (1790), at South Kensington, is a group of fashionable promenaders with the house and park for background. This was a favourite type of subject for the period. Rowlandson's *Vauxhall* preceded it

PAUL SANDBY. LADIES IN A PARK

EDWARD DAYES.   BUCKINGHAM HOUSE, ST. JAMES'S PARK

by some years. Dayes has not Rowlandson's vigour
of pen, but, gracefully drawn and quiet in colouring,
this group of figures is not lacking in spirit.

Another charming drawing is *Greenwich Hospital*,
with a party of ladies and gentlemen landing from
the river; like the other drawing it is rather pale in
tone, with reticent colour, but not without a certain
vivacity of line. The *Greenwich* is in the Whitworth Institute; and in the same gallery is a drawing
of *Vauxhall Bridge*, with a great arch spanning the
design and a group of figures below drawn with much
greater vigour. At Oxford there is a very pleasing
Durham by moonlight, in which again the span of
a bridge is the immediate feature of the design. In
the Print Room are two very large drawings, *The
Interior of St. Paul's on the Day of General Thanks-
giving* (1789) and *George III reviewing 8000 Volunteers in Hyde Park* (1799); but these are more
'important' than interesting. In 1798 Dayes exhibited a *Fall of the Angels*, followed up by other
compositions of scriptural or heroic subjects. These
were doubtless ambitious efforts. I do not know if
they survive; perhaps it is well if they do not.

Dayes was a most unequal artist; sometimes
coarse and careless, but often delicate and finely
touched. The youthful Turner made many copies
after Dayes, and it is sometimes impossible to say
whether certain drawings of old buildings in a land-

scape setting, delicately pencilled and with skies of fretted cloud, are by Turner, or Girtin, or the older draughtsman.

Dayes began as a mezzotint engraver, trained by William Pether. He wrote *Essays on Painting; Instructions for Drawing and Colouring Landscapes*, and *Professional Sketches of Modern Artists*. He committed suicide in 1804.

IV

GAINSBOROUGH; ALEXANDER AND
J. R. COZENS

PAUL SANDBY'S ambition to give his water-colours a solidity of aspect by which they might challenge comparison with oils was one which was increasingly to infect the water-colour painters, as we shall see, with the growth of exhibitions.

The artists who made their drawings for individual patrons, in whose houses these were kept in portfolios, were under no such disturbing influences. It is to this group we must now turn, for in their work flows another and a quite different stream. While Sandby and his followers were perfecting the type of drawing which has for its aim 'the view'—a kind of landscape portraiture—gaining a consummate skill in the even laying of washes and at the same time revealing to their countrymen the charm of the English country-side, and its relics of antiquity, castles and cathedrals, parks and mansions, this other group derived rather from the classic traditions of the Continent, took their subjects often from the scenery around Rome, and were

less interested in locality than in themes for com
position.

Richard Wilson is of course the chief English
master of landscape in this 'Roman' tradition. But
Wilson scarcely ever used the water-colour medium.
His drawings are almost always in black chalk on
blue or grey paper heightened with white. There is
at South Kensington a study for the 'Niobe' which
seems to be in some sort of distemper; and in the
British Museum there is a very beautiful and original
drawing of moonlight on a river, with foreground
figures on the shore, which may also be in distemper. This latter drawing belonged to Paul Sandby,
who was a great admirer of Wilson, and bought
many of his drawings when he was in straits. At
Oxford there is one of Wilson's rare drawings in
water-colour. Wilson, as Mr. Finberg has shown,
was ardently studied for a time by Turner in his
youth; by Crome also; but his influence was rather
on oil-painting than on the painters who worked in
water-colours.

His able pupil William Hodges is now remembered chiefly by his drawings made in the East and
in the South Seas, when he accompanied Captain
Cook on his second voyage in 1772–75; one of these
is in the Print Room; it is a slightly tinted monochrome. Hodges worked in India from 1778 to
1783 and published *Views in India*, engraved in

J. R. COZENS. CITARA, ON THE GULF OF SALERNO

aquatint in 1786, and *Travels in India*, 1793. Another pupil of Wilson's, Joseph Farington, has acquired far more fame a century after his death through the publication of his invaluable Diary than his drawings could ever have given him. These are usually in pen and grey wash; they have a topographical interest and a tranquil kind of merit, but of themselves have only kept his name precariously alive.

Wilson's great rival, Gainsborough, also stands alone. His natural affinity in landscape was with the painters of the Netherlands, and not at all with the Southerners, but his art became intensely personal to himself. In drawing his favourite medium was black and white chalk; but he made numerous wash-drawings of landscape. Nothing could exceed the subtlety and sureness of Gainsborough's brush in suggesting the tenderness of moisture-laden atmo-sphere and indeterminate shapes of cloud; of a like quality is his caressing touch in woodland foliage. His water-colours are mostly in tones of grey and brown; perhaps a warmth of yellow will be added, or a slight flush of gayer colour. In his later period he preferred imaginary compositions, romantic with rocks and ravines among hills, but in these he rarely used any medium but chalks, sometimes coloured. In his design there is a tendency to build on dia-gonals, which we do not find in the Claude type of design.

Gainsborough's enchanting drawings are among the most delightful things in English art. They were imitated, but fructified no school. Rowlandson no doubt took a good deal from Gainsborough in his landscape sketches; and there are direct followers like that gifted amateur Dr. Monro, but he did not as a rule paint in water-colour.

Neither Wilson nor Gainsborough, then, count for very much in the growth of the water-colour school. It is through the two Cozenses, father and son, that a new strain was introduced into English water-colours, essentially different from the home-bred Sandby traditions. Alexander Cozens' present reputation rests entirely on his monochrome compositions. There is a slight use of colour in his early drawings made in Italy: and at the Whitworth Institute is a small water-colour, but this is quite exceptional. That he painted in water-colours is certain, from his notes on method. But it is his monochromes which have survived, and for which we prize him. It is impossible, however, to neglect him in any account of the water-colour school, not only because of the stimulus he brought to it but because of the influence he exerted through his son and pupil, John Robert. I shall therefore treat of him more fully than may seem at first sight proportionate, especially as new information on his career has recently come to light.

Mr. Oppé's discovery that Richard Cozens (1674–1736), a shipbuilder, went to Russia in 1700, built many ships at St. Petersburg, moved to Archangel in 1733, and died there two years later, has inevitably cast doubt on the family tradition that Alexander was the natural son of Peter the Great and a Deptford woman. Nevertheless he seems to have been as a boy closely attached to the Court. We know this from a most interesting letter addressed to him by Beckford, in the Morrison Collection, which seems to have escaped the notice of everybody except Mr. C. F. Bell, who drew my attention to it. Beckford writes of 'your early years, when every month was marked by some great spectacle or splendid feast, when you still retain a faint idea of the gilded halls, bright lights, and a long train of nobles led by the Empress. . . . Is the mournful sight of Peter the Great's funeral forgotten, when you kissed his pale hand?'

Peter died in 1725, and the letter points to Alexander's then being a young boy, so that he may have been born, at a guess, somewhere about 1715.[1] From the same letter we learn that he was at Archangel one summer and saw the midnight sun (this strengthens the supposition that Richard Cozens the shipbuilder was his father, or at any rate his putative father), also that he went to Italy on a Swedish ship, sailing to

[1] Sir Sidney Rowlatt, a descendant of Alexander Cozens' daughter, Mrs. Roberts, kindly communicated in 1941 a pedigree of Mr. Cozens' family. This gives Alexander plainly as the son of Richard the shipbuilder and his wife Mary, daughter of Robert Davenport of Deptford, who was married in 1696 to Mary Dodd, and taken to Russia by Peter the Great. He considers 1717 to be the most likely date for Alexander's birth.

Leghorn without touching England, though he had friends there. He was in Russia in 1730, when 'Agamine the Persian'[1] presented him at St. Petersburg with a Persian drawing: but he must have been in England in 1742, as Mr. Finberg has discovered a view of Eton by him, engraved by Pine and published in that year. Could he have been at school for a time at Eton, where he was afterwards to teach drawing, after a similar appointment at Christ's Hospital? Unfortunately the complete lists of pupils do not go back so far. In the Print Room is a small pen drawing in the style of his Italian drawings, dated 1743. Perhaps he was already in Italy in that year. While at Rome he worked, as we now know, in Vernet's studio. He came back to England in 1746, as is recorded in a memorandum accompanying a book of drawings which, with many others, dropt from his saddle as he rode home through Germany that year and was recovered thirty years later by his son, who purchased it in Florence in 1776 and restored it to his father when he reached London in 1779. These drawings are now in the British Museum separately mounted.

Another book of drawings made in Rome, accompanied by memoranda on method (possibly one of the many others lost in Germany), is in the possession of Mr. Norwood Young, the artist's

[1] Probably, my colleague Mr. J. V. S. Wilkinson tells me, meant for *Agha Miyan*, both of which names are honorifics. The drawing is a sheet of studies of a love-scene, with animals on the other side, and seems to date from the early part of the eighteenth century. It is in the Duke of Hamilton's collection.

descendant, and has been published by Mr. Oppé in vol. xvi of the Walpole Society's publications. The memoranda are interesting as showing that while Cozens' main interest was already in composition, he is here concerned, in Mr. Oppé's words, with 'the actual stages at which pencil, pen, monochrome, and colour can be used in the open or in the studio in the production of what he would call landscape views'. He insists on study and on accuracy of detail; and he sets out a variety of methods to be used according to the aim the artist has before him—topographical delineation or atmospheric effect—whether painting directly from Nature or in the studio, etc. We note that Method 6 begins 'With Water Collors 30 in all in bottles in frame &c. without drawing begin at once ye distance only ye general Masses then ye particulars'.

The set of drawings in the Museum, already mentioned, is more important than the studies in Mr. Young's book. They are mostly from Rome and the Campagna, but there is a series of small sketches done in the island of Elba. Some are in pen-and-ink, neatly shaded with parallel strokes, some in grey wash, some in tinted water-colour—delicate and pleasing. The artist is obviously interested in the actual scene before him, and is often profuse in rather careful detail. The most striking sketch is an effect of sun bursting from clouds with long rays

37

over a stretch of country sloping to a white sea. Another drawing is elaborately squared-out, apparently for enlargement.

As we have seen, Alexander Cozens settled in England in 1746. He began to exhibit in 1760. In the mid-eighteenth century, as we know from the Farington Diaries, there were very few artists in the country who taught drawing; besides Sandby, the master most in repute was John Melchair, who settled in Oxford about 1760. Cozens taught drawing at Eton, 1763–68,[1] also at Bath and in London. He revisited the Continent, 1764. The kind of landscape for which he is famous is very different from that of the early drawings made in Italy. In *A New Method of assisting the Invention in Drawing Original Compositions of Landscape* he describes how he accidentally hit on the device of working up a casual blot of ink or sepia into the composition its shapes suggested. And he tells of his joy in discovering that Leonardo had been before him, with his advice to study the rough texture of an old wall for suggestions of landscape form; he would have rejoiced still more if he had known that a Chinese painter had been before Leonardo with similar advice.

So Cozens would use the hints to invention given by his blots. 'Blot-master to the Town' he was dubbed

---

[1] According to the *Dictionary of National Biography*. He was certainly teaching at Eton, Mr. R. A. Austen Leigh informs me, in 1766.

by the bilious Edward Dayes; and those who prized skill and patience above all things in a drawing thought Cozens a charlatan. Yet Cozens thought a great deal about the principles of design. He was probably conscious that he applied himself too much to abstract theory, and resorted to the stimulus of accident in order to freshen his imagination. His sepia drawings show a curious affinity to certain schools of Chinese landscape. I exhibited two of them in Japan, and the Japanese painters and critics were astonished by the close similarity of aim.

In the Print Room there is an album of Sundry Studies of Landscape Composition, which seem to have been made for the guidance of pupils, probably for his son John Robert, to whom they once belonged. The album begins with some pages divided up into small compartments, illustrating 'Principles of Land-skip' in 'slight' and 'rich' composition; 'Historical Landskip of the Egyptian and of the Grecian Age; Historical Landskip of the Roman and of the Modern Age; Circumstances of Landskip'. Smile as we may at this legendary codification, we perceive the bent of Alexander's mind and his love of *a priori* principles. Between 1771 and 1785 he published several treatises, among others *Principles of Beauty relative to the Human Head* (1778).

The remainder of the album just mentioned is filled with sketches for compositions, nearly all drawn

39

with a brush in very thick black ink or in bistre.
There is great variety in the motives of design. Now
we look out from under over-arching trees into sunlight; now a single great pine dominates a solitude;
or the prospect is of desert plains rising to a remote
hill; or a vista down a road between dense woods. In
one sketch the whole foreground is a swampy thicket
with intricate foliage beyond which is sunlight and
a hilly distance. There are reminiscences of Nemi
Lake cupped in its deep hollow (the motive recurs
in Cozens' work), and others which seem suggested
by the land-locked bay of Porto Lungone in Elba,
of which he had made several drawings on the spot.
Most striking of all is a sketch of a sort of estuary
between rocky mountains, the scale of which is im-
pressively suggested by a tiny ship upon the water.

It is brush drawings of this kind, larger and less
impetuously summary in technique, by which Alexander Cozens is now remembered. With a combination of ink and bistre he could suggest rich colour.
They are sometimes singularly Chinese in conception
and style: but in his severer moods he will at times
recall, more than any other European artist, the
paintings and etchings of Hercules Seghers, who
had a passion for the bareness of rocks and the solitude of mountains. Alexander married a sister of
Robert Edge Pine, and it was mainly through his
son John Robert that his influence on the whole

landscape school was indirectly exerted. He died in Duke Street, Piccadilly, in 1786.

Alexander Cozens was a Romantic such as only the Age of Reason could have provoked into existence. His *Historical Principles of Landscape* might suggest a pedant; but actually he seems to have been inflammable of mind and of a temperament that recalls the youthful Shelley and his circle. He remains shadowy as regards the facts of his life; but a series of letters to him from William Beckford show, as in a mirror, the kind of man he was.

How Beckford and Alexander came to meet we do not know. They were intimate before 1780, when Beckford was twenty, and Cozens must have been more than forty years the elder; no doubt he wore for Beckford a halo of Oriental romance, but the young man treats him as a contemporary. 'No one understands me but Cozens', he cries. Like Beckford, Alexander was exotic, made a cult of emotion, and suffered from fits of dejection as well as from 'the delightful delirium which none but souls like ours experience'. 'How firmly am I resolved to be a child for ever!' 'Be assured you will find me ever the same romantic being': in such a strain does the young man write to his elderly but enthusiastic confidant.

Beckford does not seem to have found the younger Cozens, John Robert, at all so sympathetic as his father, though interested in his drawings. The son was evidently less outwardly responsive, certainly not at all ebullient, but quiet and reserved in manner.

John Cozens was born (probably) in 1752, and was his father's pupil. He began to exhibit as early as 1767. In 1776 he went to Switzerland with Richard Payne-Knight: Beckford, who was then only sixteen, had not, it would seem, appeared on the scene as yet. Payne-Knight was afterwards to become an eminent arbiter of taste, famous for his splendid collections, bequeathed to the British Museum, also for his condemnation of the Elgin Marbles in opposition to B. R. Haydon. At this time he was a young dilettante of twenty-six. He was interested in landscape, and later on, in 1794, was to publish a poem on the subject, inspired by hostility to the ideas of 'Capability' Brown and opening:

How best to bid the verdant Landscape rise,
To please the fancy, and delight the eyes . . .

Payne-Knight was a man of his period.

Apparently before starting abroad Cozens sent in his one contribution to a Royal Academy exhibition. This was a landscape with Hannibal crossing the Alps. It profoundly impressed the youthful Turner when he saw it later; he said he learnt more from it than from any picture he had seen till then. This picture may still exist. It disappeared about 1876, but is remembered vaguely by some of the artist's descendants, one of whom, Mr. Dalhousie Young, wrote to me in 1916 that his 'recollection is that there were mountains and soldiers and elephants, one of which was falling down a ravine, and Hannibal in purple on horseback'. It is said to have been in oils. An Indian-ink drawing of the subject, which I have seen, is apparently by Cozens and may represent an alternative composition.

A series of sketches done on the spot, chiefly Swiss, which was the result of Cozens' first tour of the Continent, belonged to Payne-Knight, and, after passing through other hands, was broken up. Twenty-four are now in the British Museum. The drawings are not superficially striking. There is a lack of emphasis and contrast, a sort of pervading pallor in the atmosphere, and sometimes a clumsiness in handling. One would say that they were anything but clever; yet, more closely studied, they betray an unobtrusive subtlety and skill. It is wonderful what value Cozens gives to white paper left blank among the washes of subtle greys: snow gleams out among the clouds. But the technique interests less than the qualities of mind and feeling that come through the imperfect means of execution. What is it that these drawings reflect? No pleasure (one would say) in the artist's skill, no concern to render the faithful aspect of a place, and yet no exploitation of the scene before the eyes, to turn it into a fine 'effect'. Nor is there any effort to seize and set down

43

the structure of the rocks and mountains. What is communicated is feeling, but feeling of a rare kind. It is a passion for solitude: *O beata solitudo, O sola beatitudo!* It is an exquisite sense for the marvellous mountain-stillness. The world is removed; the terror and glory of Alp and glacier veil themselves; the infinitely remote, the impalpable, a mingling of cloud and snow, a suspension of motion, attract the surrendered spirit. Nothing of the picturesque, nothing of romantic 'Horrour', appears. Few indeed would have chosen such motives as Cozens often chooses; water, rock, and cloud, without arresting play of light and shadow, without enlivening features in the foreground. It is as if his spirit sought to steep itself in baths of silence.

Of course it must be remembered that these are not finished drawings. The drawings made from these sketches have no pen-work, and are more 'composed'. Still, the sketches have the value of giving Cozens' immediate impressions. One of the finished drawings, *Interlaken*, may be studied in the same collection; it was bequeathed by Mr. Salting. Here Cozens' mastery of his medium is apparent. From a flat meadow, beyond which a stream runs under trees, the eye is carried up the valley to the snow-covered Jungfrau range; but their sharpness is mitigated by the veils of atmosphere, for from the obscured sun only faint rays stream out over the valley. In the quiet scheme of colour a tender blue tells beautifully.

Cozens was away from England on this tour till 1779. He was in Florence, as we have seen, in 1776. In the Print Room are a drawing of *Etna from Grotta del Capro*, which was dated on the former mount May 1777, and a few other Sicilian drawings. But he does not seem to have continued in the company of Payne-Knight, who travelled in Sicily with the German artist Hackert and the English amateur, Charles Gore, and whose diary on the tour was translated by Goethe. Cozens returned to Rome, and was there in 1778. He was to be in Rome again four years later; and there is some confusion between the drawings made on these two different occasions.

Cozens' second Continental tour was made in company with Beckford. They started in May 1782. Beckford had come of age in the previous autumn. His fortune was immense, but all the normal tastes, habits, and ambitions of an English country gentleman were hateful to him. In 1780 he had been sent abroad to distract him from a violent love affair; and now, two years later, another tour was prescribed by the family council. Beckford had just composed his famous Oriental romance *Vathek* and was in a state of feverish sensibility.

The party travelled in princely state; in the first carriage were Beckford and his ex-tutor, in the second

Cozens and a musician, Mr. Burton. They passed rapidly through the Low Countries to Cologne, thence to Nassereit in the Tyrol, where Cozens began to make sketches. The sketches were made in books, seven of which are preserved in Hamilton Palace; and from them we can trace the route followed by the travellers from Innsbruck to Verona and Padua. After a hasty visit to Venice and the Euganean Hills they finally reached Rome on 25th June. On 6th July Beckford pushed on to Naples, where the party broke up. Beckford went home to get married, leaving Cozens, who spent the autumn in the neighbourhood of Naples. On 8th December he started for Rome and probably stayed there for some months, though we hear of him at Naples with Sir William Hamilton in April 1783 playing the violoncello. 'He has made some charming sketches', writes Sir William, 'but I see by his book he is indolent as ever.' In spite of his indolence and the distractions of music, the finished water-colours made from the sketches on this tour make an imposing array; and there were certainly days on which he worked with feverish industry.

It was not for nothing that he was his father's pupil. We see how little he was tied to variations on a single formula of composition. We recognise hints from Alexander's inventive projects. The relation of dark to light, of the foreground to the distance, is

46

constantly changing. Sometimes, as in the *Rome from the Villa Mellini*, of which there is a version in the British Museum and another at Cambridge, you might think that Cozens' aim was a classical serenity of design and atmosphere: but more often, as with some of the drawings of the Lake of Nemi and the Lake of Albano, there is grandeur of gloom and mass. The *Tomb of the Horatii and Curiatii* at South Kensington, with its boughs of foliage drooping into the design (a characteristic Cozens motive), seems steeped in a kind of impersonal melancholy: the *Valley with Winding Streams* in the same museum is infinitely tender. In other drawings there is something tumultuous in the broken light and shade. The skies are often magnificent; they partake of the character of the design, now infinitely luminous, now charged with menace and oppressive cloud. No previous master of landscape had painted a finer sky than that which piles its clouds above the dark woods in *The Belvedere at Rome* in the Birmingham Gallery or the menacing wreaths of storm that hang above the *Paestum* (now in the Oldham Gallery). In this last design the two great temples are no longer classic remains, themes of interest to the archaeologist; they have become hollow and forlorn symbols of mortality, with sultry wind blowing through their gaunt shells and over the utter solitude that surrounds them, while confused shapes of cloud slowly impend as the

47

sky darkens above. The theme has become universal. Still more intimately in Cozens' mood is the *Ruined Aqueducts in the Campagna* in the Barnard Collection; an immense emptiness, a veiled sun paling the sky above a mass of ghostly cloud, a few mouldering towers and the long line of broken aqueduct in the distance.

But in other drawings there is agitation and contrast, broken lights and darks; notably in the impressive mountain forms that ascend, abrupt and overwhelming, above the town and still waters at the foot of them, in *Citara on the Gulf of Salerno* in the Girtin Collection. A drawing at Cambridge essays the violence of storm at sea and sweeping volleys of rain, also in the Gulf of Salerno; not quite successfully perhaps; but, as always, Cozens makes his skies, whether peaceful or tormented, an integral part of the design pervading the whole. In another drawing of an Alpine valley (known in several versions) the sky is of the most complex texture, with interwoven shadows and breaking beams of light. Grey, blue, and green are the prevailing colours; there is seldom more than a touch of warmer hues; but who would have them otherwise? The tones in the finest drawings are of great subtlety and depth. Two drawings are exceptional in colour; both are in Mr. Girtin's collection. One is a *Scene in the Euganean Hills*, with light breaking through haze and disclosing hills of

J. R. COZENS.   LAKE ALBANO: AFTER SUNSET

THOMAS ROWLANDSON.   SKATERS ON THE SERPENTINE

a blue (perhaps cobalt) such as Cozens seldom or never uses elsewhere. The other is a *Tivoli*, with strong contrasts of tone and again an unusual, though a different, blue.

In the winter of 1922–23 an exhibition of J. R. Cozens' work was held at the Burlington Fine Arts Club. Many of his finest drawings were assembled on the walls; and it was possible to realise the range and depth of an artist who is all too little known to his countrymen. If Constable's often-quoted, enthusiastic phrase be found extravagant, yet before such drawings as the Nemi in the Lloyd Collection, so luminous, so tender in its tones, we can echo his saying 'Cozens is all poetry'. Cozens often essays more than his technical powers suffice for; he is never too easily master of his material, though he is masterly often in his composition, and in his use of his medium. But above and beyond all other qualities, it is the mind and feeling in his art that give it power and distinction.

Of many of Cozens' designs there are several versions. He used the material gathered on his Swiss and Italian tours for finished water-colours made afterwards in England. Of English subjects few seem to be known; but he painted in Windsor Forest; and a fine *Greenwich*, with an empty sky, was shown at the Walker Galleries a few years ago; it was a subject in which he could find something of the classic features

49

of the Italian scene. No drawing of his dated later than 1792 appears to be known. His mind probably was then beginning to fail.

On 26th January 1794 Farington heard from Sir George Beaumont that Cozens was 'paralytic to a degree that has incapacitated him'. In February he was 'confined under the care of Dr. Monro, who has no expectation of his recovery'. A little later we learn: 'Cozens' disorder is described to be a total decay of the nervous system. He appeared to be of a silent, hesitating disposition, and of grave manners. Some time since a total change took place. He became childishly noisy and talkative on trifles.' The exact year of his death is not quite certain, but is generally stated to have been 1799.

The importance of the two Cozenses in the water-colour school is partly the fact that they brought it into touch with the main European traditions of landscape and saved it from provincial obscurity, and perhaps still more that they did not merely produce a derivative from Claude and Gaspar Poussin but originated a landscape art of their own, stimulated by thought and expressive of emotion. Lack of original ideas, incapacity to coördinate ideas, and laborious tameness of execution; these are the besetting weaknesses on which Alexander laid his finger.

WILLIAM PARS AND FRANCIS TOWNE

BETWEEN Cozens' two visits to Rome, another English painter, Francis Towne, joined his friend William Pars, who had settled there in 1775 and who was to die there in 1782 in the prime of his life.

Pars was at this time the better known of the two. Born in 1742, he had won a reputation by his drawings made in Greece for the Dilettanti Society, which were engraved and published in Chandler and Revett's *Ionian Antiquities* in 1769. These water-colours are in the British Museum. They are very accomplished, and the figures are as well drawn as the landscapes. Pars practised as a portrait painter, I suppose in water-colours (some were miniatures), and in the Print Room is a rather charming water-colour portrait of Miss Cronin of Killarney. This is only slightly tinted; but the Ionian drawings show a fairly full range of colour, much more than Cozens was to use. One of them is unfinished, and we can see Pars' method of working. There is no grey underpainting, the local colours are laid on directly. Pars is perfectly master of what he sets out to do, composes agreeably, and always keeps before him the archaeological interest of his subjects. He works with a cool mind and seems never to be visited by strange moods, or stirred in his profounder feelings. We are therefore not greatly interested in him as a landscape painter.

Pars returned to England in 1766. His brother Henry Pars, eight years older than himself, kept a drawing-school in the Strand for over forty years, very well known in its time. William Pars next went abroad with Lord Palmerston, who took him through Switzerland and the Tyrol to Rome. The series of Swiss drawings which were engraved, and some of which are in the Print Room, are less interesting in themselves than for their contrast with those of Cozens and of Towne. It must be remembered that they are earlier in time; they were perhaps the earliest revelation of the high Alps to the untravelled English public when they were exhibited in London in 1771. Revelation is, however, too emotional a word for these calm transcripts of mountain wilderness, of contorted masses and pinnacles of ice, which Pars delineates with the same undisturbed competence that he would have brought to the drawing of a country seat in the Home Counties of England. Groups of peasants, hardy and contented, enliven his foregrounds and counteract the oppression of solitude.

Francis Towne, when he died, wished that his

drawings of Rome might repose in the British Museum along with the drawings of his friend Pars. The two had been attached to each other, it seems, from the days when they were fellow-pupils at Shipley's school. But Towne, who was the elder by a couple of years—he was born in 1739 or 1740—was of a very different temperament. Another friend, John Downman, drew him in early middle life. There is something almost feminine in the look of this profile, at once sensitive and sensuous, with the large eyes and the full lips; a nature innocent and unworldly, one would say, self-centred, very serious, with no protective armour of humorous detachment, yet capable of concentrated purpose. His nerves were excitable; he could not drink tea in the afternoon, he told Farington, because it prevented him sleeping at night.

Mr. Oppé has collected all the known facts of Towne's life and recorded them in the Walpole Society's eighth volume. We do not know where he was born, but though trained in London at Shipley's school with Pars, Cosway, and Ozias Humphry, he was closely connected with Exeter—he lived there for a time from 1767—and his patrons were mostly West-country people. Throughout his life Towne painted in oils as well as in water-colours, and his early drawings were mostly studies for oil pictures. In 1777 he made a tour in Wales. In 1780 he went to Rome, returning home through Switzerland in 1781 in company with 'Warwick' Smith. For fourteen years he lived in London, wintering in Exeter. In 1786 he toured the English Lakes. In 1800 he married a young French dancer, who died in 1808, the year after he had taken a house in London. He died in 1816.

Wales, Rome, Switzerland; it was these which gave him the most momentous experiences of his life, and drew out his finest gifts. The Welsh drawings are, according to Mr. Oppé, rather timid in the attack on the subjects, whether mountains or buildings. Some are fully coloured, others only a monochrome preparation. But in the austere *Salmon-Leap* in the Merivale Collection, reproduced by Mr. Oppé, we already find that strong feeling for the bare bones of rock, that sense of mass and structure, which was to inspire his later work and which places him apart among the painters of his time.

In the long series of Roman drawings in the Print Room we find this love of form and structure for their own sake combined, as it was more fully and felicitously in Cotman later, with a strong instinct for pattern in colour. All these seventy-four drawings are carefully dated, the hours they occupied being often recorded; many were 'drawn on the spot', and perhaps this was the case with all. Approaching Rome, Towne seems first to be charmed

with the spacious and luminous air over the wide
Campagna traversed by roads that wind from the
distant hills. But in the city itself it is the stupendous
mass of the Roman ruins that absorbs him, ruins so
vast that they seem, with their overgrowth of bush
and tree, to assume the character of mountains. We
are struck by his extraordinary originality. Form
and colour appeal to him for their own sake, almost
as they might to an artist of our own day. There is
no oppression of tradition, derived from Claude and
his followers; if there are any traces of his predecessors' influence, they are hardly perceptible.
Towne sees with his own vision. Sometimes the
scene is bathed in a warm glow so that we seem to
feel the heat of an afternoon's decline; yet he is not
interested in atmosphere. His trees with their long
snake-like boughs, their flat breadths of foliage,
seem incapable of being stirred by any wind; he
seems little concerned with the movement of things,
he paints water without life. Softness and the tender
gradations of gloom are not for him; he loves the
linear definition, and rarely lays aside his pen. But
confronted with the crumbling masses of the Baths
of Caracalla, of the ancient Walls of Rome, of the
Colosseum, his mind stirs as to a challenge; the
memorableness of his designs bears witness to the
emotion they evoked. He plots broad shadows inter-
sected by planes of light; he gives to the bulk of

shadowed masses an almost sinister force and weight, accentuated by the clear evening light beyond them. Towne contrasts warm and cool colours as Cozens never did; there are drawings in this series, especially two of the Baths of Caracalla, which remind me, rather, of those masterly simplifications of colour-design which forty years later Hokusai was to achieve in his landscape woodcuts. Not that Towne is an assured master; attempting to reduce too complex elements to his scheme he often fails. Always using a pen outline, he has a formula for the edges of his foliage which at times becomes a little absurd, though it seems of little consequence in the total effect of his broadly mapped designs. There is one drawing of Nemi, almost a monochrome, in which the woods surrounding the lake seem as if their masses were sculptured out of the same solid substance as the hills. In another drawing of a Roman scene, trees in deepest shadow, with light seen beneath their foliage, make a strong mass in a very original design.

Much of technical shortcoming will be forgiven to one who can at times stimulate us by that unexpectedness which is so precious a quality in art. Often one feels in Towne's designs a certain strangeness, which detaches him from his century.

Towne stayed on in Rome and Naples till August 1781, and then turned northward in company with 'Warwick' Smith. This painter, born in Cumberland in 1749, had worked on topographical lines in England. He was taken to Italy by the Earl of Warwick and was there by 1778, which is the date of a drawing of Vesuvius in the British Museum. His many Italian water-colours became so popular that he was known also as 'Italian Smith'. Towne's work not being known, Smith was supposed to have introduced fuller and brighter tones of colour. He had no particular style, and our interest in him is faint. He lived till 1831. A series of his views in the English Lakes was engraved.

On Lake Como Towne made a drawing which is as unlike the usual conception of Italian lake scenery as could be imagined. At the end of a long stretch of the lake a great cumulus cloud focusses attention. A long ridge of hills at the right sloping down to the water cuts off the sunset light which flushes the edges of the cloud, outlined as usual with the pen. All is definite and severe, instead of scenic and luxurious. It is the distinction of Towne that his mind is never content with the surface of things; it is their structural relations that he seeks to grasp.

Remarkable as the Roman drawings are, they are less remarkable than the Swiss drawings first made known to the public and appraised at their true value by Mr. Oppé. Here again Towne's sense for structure, and his linear definition, are manifest; but something is added: on his impressionable spirit the mountains, in their starkness, impose a fascination mingled with terror, such as the ancient masses of crumbling Rome could not evoke.

This was an age in which Cowper found a journey over the South Downs from Chichester a terrifying adventure. Towne, a febrile spirit, if not so tremulous as Cowper, had infinitely more reason for discovering terror in the icy secrets of the Alps, which his friend Pars had looked on with so placid an eye. How different is Towne's vision from either Pars' or Cozens'! Cozens had wandered in the Alpine valleys, immersing himself in congenial solitude; if he lifted his eyes, he saw the gleam of snowy summits from the floating veils of cloud; he saw the great peaks in the beauty of remoteness, like apparitions in a dream. Now and then he came to closer quarters, yet we feel that he preferred them in the distance. But Towne was drawn with fascinated vision to confront these stupendous shapes in their nearness and reality.

Two drawings of the Swiss series are especially notable. Both are of the sources of the Arveiron, and are upright in their proportion. In one, two shoulders of the mountain slope down, utterly bare, from the left, in grand curves; crossing them, in front, is the curve of the glacier from the right. Beyond the crushed ice of the glacier one divines a tremendous hollow. The stark simplicity of the design, with its cold blue and gleaming white, is singular in the art

of the period. It is reproduced as the frontispiece
to this book. The other drawing is more complex,
though it has the same play of curve against curve.
The glacier with its crawling ice and blue-lipped
cavern is here the main feature of the design; and the
crushed chaos in which it ends, and the dragon-like
form of its descent are pictured with a sense of enormous latent menace. This drawing is now in the
Victoria and Albert Museum, where also are two of
the water-colours made in the English Lake District
in 1786.

With Towne may be mentioned his friend and
pupil, John White Abbot (*b.* 1763, *d.* after 1827)
who followed his style in water-colours very closely,
but was fond, in his later years at any rate, of introducing figures from classic story and pastoral.

While Italy and Greece were drawing English
artists to paint classic landscapes and remains of
antiquity, others were journeying farther afield and
out of Europe. The drawings made in the South Seas
and in India by William Hodges have been mentioned already. Thomas Daniell (1749–1840) went
to India in 1784 with his nephew William. He stayed
ten years in the country and with his nephew's help
prepared a large work called *Oriental Scenery*, completed in 1808. The drawings were mostly in monochrome or lightly tinted; they were exhibited lately

at the Walker Galleries in Bond Street, and are sometimes of real charm, light and delicate in touch. William Daniell (1769–1837) is known for his Oriental drawings and also for a work in four volumes *A Voyage round Great Britain*, excellent drawings of the coast engraved in aquatint; but the drawings for this work seem to have disappeared. His brother Samuel Daniell (1775–1811) sailed to South Africa; he made many good drawings there, and went on to Ceylon, where he died.

William Alexander (1767–1816) went with Lord Macartney's embassy to China in 1792; his water-colours of Chinese scenes are admirable; he also drew English landscapes. He was the first Keeper of Prints and Drawings in the British Museum. Thomas Hickey also went with Lord Macartney's embassy and painted scenes in China in a somewhat similar style to that of Alexander.

FIGURE PAINTERS: ROWLANDSON

BETWEEN Hogarth and Rowlandson there are few figure painters who made more than an occasional use of water-colour, and that usually as a preliminary study for an oil-picture: the drawing by Francis Cotes already mentioned (p. 18) is an example.

John Collet, however, who was born about 1725 and died in 1780, made a name as a minor successor to Hogarth; his *Asylum for the Deaf* in the Victoria and Albert Museum is very much in his master's vein; and he also made a number of small drawings in water-colours and pen, country scenes, landscapes, and idylls with a humorous flavour. Paul Sandby, as we have seen, had a real gift for figure-drawing and grouping, but his figures usually remain accessory to his landscapes. Hieronymus Grimm made a number of large drawings of a similar type, with more incident. At the Whitworth Institute is a water-colour, *Sunday Evening at Bagnigge Wells*, an animated company of men and women, by John Sanders (*b.* about 1750), anticipating the type of drawing which

Rowlandson in his *Vauxhall Gardens*, and Dayes in his *Promenade, Buckingham House*, were afterwards to make into little masterpieces of their kind.

But these names are unimportant compared with those of Rowlandson and of Blake, who were almost exact contemporaries. They died in the same year, 1827; Rowlandson was born in 1756, Blake in 1757. In spirit and in choice of subject they were poles apart; they were alike only in an immense productiveness continued till death. They are the two chief figure-draughtsmen of the water-colour school in the eighteenth and early nineteenth centuries; and, though so utterly different, both used the medium in much the same way, as draughtsmen rather than as painters, though this is only partially true of Blake.

Thomas Rowlandson occupies a peculiar and isolated place in English art. In his own day he had immense popularity. His drawings and prints were in all the print-sellers' shops. His gift was a kind of running fountain, purveyor of laughter to the average man, who saw nothing in him more than the reflection of his own tastes and discerned none of his real qualities as an artist. A few collectors were the exception. To the nineteenth century he no doubt seemed merely coarse, especially as his prints, from which nearly all the charm of his drawings has evaporated, were what he was chiefly known by. And as he did not compete with the oil painters, and stood quite apart from what was considered to be the true water-colour tradition, he was till lately hardly regarded seriously, though I believe he has long been appreciated in France. While the works of showy and superficial portrait painters like Hoppner were fetching great sums at auctions, drawings by Rowlandson, worth infinitely more as art, were in cheap esteem. And it is no doubt inevitable that so enormous a production as Rowlandson's should have counted against him.

The facts of his life are few and soon told. He was born in 1756. He entered as a boy the schools of the Royal Academy, but in 1771, when he was not yet sixteen, he went to Paris and studied in a drawing-school there for two years. He had a French aunt. But he remained obstinately English, and French people to him were usually objects of ridicule. In Paris perhaps he learnt to draw with more science and more animation than was then prevalent in England; at any rate, on his returning to London and re-entering the Academy schools he became famous for his nude studies, being even thought to rival J. H. Mortimer, the idol of the last generation of students. He began to exhibit at the Royal Academy in 1775, sending a drawing of Samson and Delilah. For a few years he exhibited portraits, no doubt drawings. There is a charming example of his later portraiture in the Print Room, George

Morland, elegant in a green coat, standing in an easy attitude in front of a mantelpiece. About 1780 he found his true vein, and the torrential flow from his inventive pencil scarcely ceased till his death in 1827.

His perennial and inexhaustible theme was the life around him, life as he saw it. He passed for a caricaturist; it is the term still commonly applied to him. There is an element in his art of caricature, but it is far from being its essence. He was quite incapable of the pungent criticism, the penetrating seriousness, underlying the satiric drawings, with their light washes of tender colour, of Max Beerbohm. He was no critic; he had hardly a 'point of view'. Nor was he a social satirist, like Hogarth, nor a political satirist, like Gillray. He had none of the indignation of the one, or the ferocity of the other. He accepted life as it was in the England of the days of George III and the Regency, totally uncritical of its boisterous and brutal aspects. Careless of money —he squandered in gambling a small fortune left him by the French aunt, and other legacies—fond of wine and women, a lover of gay company, of inns and travel, he was distinguished from a multitude of other roysterers only by his marvellous gift and the amazing industry in which it overflowed. There was even a callous and brutal side to his nature, characteristic enough of the period, yet disconcerting to those for whom his drawings are a delight. But whatever he did, he enjoyed. An abounding and insatiable gusto of enjoyment pervades his work.

Mr. Oppé's book,[1] with its many reproductions, gives a good idea of Rowlandson's various kinds of theme and treatment. There is indeed plenty of variety, though there is no growth or development after the artist's style was once formed. As Mr. Oppé has shown, there is no perceptible decline either, such as one might expect from so excessive and facile a production: 'there is bad work at every period', but admirable work produced at the same time, even in the last years.

In Mr. Marsh's collection there is a drawing of workmen busy among the débris of the Savoy Palace, the ruins of which were sedulously drawn by the youthful Turner and Girtin. Rowlandson's drawing, with its groups of active workmen, is amusing and delightful; but when we place beside it an early Girtin, with its feeling for solemn shadow, we realise how utterly uninfluenced Rowlandson was by the younger generation of water-colour painters, and continued to be long years after Girtin had transfigured the art of the topographers; also how alien to him was any expression of deep emotion. But it is just this absence of emotion which gives so

[1] A. P. Oppé, *Thomas Rowlandson: his Drawings and Water-Colours.* The Studio, Ltd., 1923.

65

adorable a quality of lightness to his work. His few excursions into the serious or the tragic are unfortunate and may be disregarded. It is the surface of life, the shifting, many-coloured crowd of human beings, sunshine on water and foliage, that is Rowlandson's concern. That is, as far as subject is concerned. But we are not really interested in any of the myriad figures that people his radiant drawings; not at least for their own sake. It is something quite different that enchants the eye; and this something is not at all superficial, it is one of the rarest of gifts —that of creating a kind of melodious play in the relations between the forms that animate the scenes; so that, with the seeming ease of the swift pen-line, a whole crowd of figures, often in violent agitation, young bucks, slim graceful girls, pretty buxom women, crapulous old men, paunchy grotesques, street ruffians, children, are all caught up as by a compelling tune into a flowing arabesque, and are magically translated from the world of fact into the artist's world of line and colour.

Those who dwell on Rowlandson's human types, or on the incidents providing his ostensible motives— his humour is mostly of the elementary kind—miss the whole point of him. At bottom he is a lyrist. Among other draughtsmen he engages us at once with the singing voice, the dancing feet. Had he had the gifts which we fail to find in him—emotion, sympathy, indignation, searching observation—he would not be what he is, probably he would be less, not greater. At any rate, his gift is unique; let us be glad of him, rather than deplore his deficiencies.

Where the original water-colour of *Vauxhall Gardens* is, I do not know, if indeed it still exists:[1] but it may well have been, as it has been called, Rowlandson's masterpiece, to judge from Jukes's aquatint published in 1785. Debucourt's famous and delightful colour-print, *Promenade de la Galerie du Palais Royal*, was published in 1787, and is said to have been inspired by emulation with the *Vauxhall Gardens*. Rarely does Rowlandson bestow such pains upon a composition or aim at so solid an effect—though the pen-work of the original must have been light and lively. The night-effect and artificial lighting give a logical force and depth, and the contrasts are not too violent. Elsewhere, where he attempts to give relief by grey shadow in daylight scenes, the effect is seldom felicitous; something of the characteristic gaiety seems to go, the vivacity of the pen-line seems obscured. Perhaps we enjoy the artist most in his spontaneous sketches with their vivid line, sweet rhythms, and delicate flush of colour. Yet it is to be deplored that very few of the finest draw-

---

[1] The drawing of Vauxhall Gardens was re-discovered in a village shop in Hertfordshire in the summer of 1945. Shortly afterwards it changed hands at Christie's for 2,600 guineas. It is reproduced in *The Connoisseur* for September 1945.

6

ings of the more elaborate sort are in our public collections; some of the best are in America. Mr. Tonks's often-reproduced *Exhibition Starecase*, engraved about 1800, is one of the most brilliant of Rowlandson's works; an unusually original design, farcical and coarse in motive, but the absurd cascade of figures is sketched in with such exuberant swiftness, the reed-pen creates so joyously, that the elements are forgotten in the exhilarating whole.

In 1784 Rowlandson made a large drawing of great beauty, *Skating on the Serpentine*. This is in private hands and in a brilliant state of preservation. The London Museum has a replica of two years later date, inferior to the other. The subject, with its gaily animated crowd of all classes, its mishaps and collisions, is one after Rowlandson's heart. What is unusual with him is the truth of atmosphere; the bare trees dimmed in the distance by the misty air, the pallor of winter sunshine, the feeling of frost, all are conveyed with an intimate subtlety. And in the mid-distance, half-hidden by the crowd, are three young skaters, arm in arm, gliding away into the pearly haze, as if they with their delight in life and motion embodied the essence of Rowlandson the artist, hidden from and disguised by the uproarious world.

In Rowlandson's landscapes, of which there are so many, there is rarely any touch of intimacy, rarely much attempt at atmosphere. He is a draughtsman, not a painter. Like Gainsborough, he has his chosen conventions, which often become, especially in his trees, a facile formula. What is notable in his best landscape drawings, which are delicious things, is their amazing economy of expression. So few lines, so much life.

Rowlandson made a number of tours on the Continent and drew many views of foreign streets and architecture: in these there is always his charm of line; but he is happier at home in England, especially in his drawings of seaports, with calm sea lying under luminous haze and casually stranded boats.

During his life-time, no doubt, Rowlandson's popularity came from the drawings which could be more definitely labelled caricatures, whether social or political. Isaac Cruikshank (*b.* about 1756, *d.* about 1811) was on this side in some sort a rival: his drawings in water-colours are vigorous but without the underlying beauty of Rowlandson's pen-work. He is now almost forgotten. His more famous son George sometimes used water-colours in his drawings with agreeable animation: there is a charming *Figures on Ramsgate Pier* in the Print Room.

Here may be mentioned an artist of distinguished talent, John Augustus Atkinson, born in 1775, who was taken as a child to St. Petersburg, enjoyed the imperial patronage and returned to England in 1801. He published books with many coloured plates on the costume, etc., of Russia, and a similar 'Picturesque Representation' of English life. His water-colours show a fresh and vivacious use of the medium.

James Ward (1769–1859), who belongs to the Rowlandson and Morland group, an artist whose fame has never equalled his deserts, made, I believe, no regular practice of water-colours; but his coloured drawings show real feeling for the medium. A brush drawing of a farm girl with a small boy, in the Print Room, is delightfully handled. Julius Caesar Ibbetson (1759–1817), like Ward, made his chief reputation by his paintings of animals—cattle and pigs especially. His water-colours are of the kind of subject painted in oils by Morland; farm scenes, landscapes with cattle, gipsies, etc. Some good examples are in the Print Room and at South Kensington.

VII

BLAKE

BLAKE bursts into the mental atmosphere of his age with the energy of an explosion and the strangeness of an apparition. But his strangeness has become less strange, now that we can understand him better. Too long regarded merely as an eccentric, who painted wild visions of his own, he has his significance less in his isolation in his own time than in his effort to rediscover the imaginative tradition of medieval England. His contemporaries, in so far as they attempted imaginative art, were content with the conceptions of picture-making in fashion, derived from Bolognese Eclectics or from the Venetians. Blake's admiration was all for Michelangelo, of whom he had no first-hand knowledge, and he consciously imitated him; but he derived far more from the half-conscious saturation of his mind with the medieval sculpture which he had studied in his youth, and which provided models more truly congenial to his instinct for form. His imagination was all his own. He took his subjects from Milton and the Bible, avoiding classic mythology, but interpreted the given themes afresh, in his own way; and he invented a mythology of his own. But he always thought of himself as an English artist. One of his favourite books was Milton's *History of England*, especially the early legendary part, and like Milton he was proud of his race, though he deplored that in this country there was no opportunity for painting heroic or religious compositions on the walls of churches and public buildings. He would have liked to paint in fresco, though he had no knowledge of the process. He tried oils, but was disappointed with the dead effect of the pigment when it dried, and reviled the medium ever after. In any case he never had the luxury of a studio to paint in. He painted some works in a sort of tempera, but these have all cracked and blackened. Almost the whole of his work is in water-colours.

Blake's first works in water-colour were in the vein of Mortimer, their subjects being taken from English history. They are in Indian ink, tinted over with colour, and there is little in them to disengage them from their period. In some other drawings, made a little later, Blake's peculiar imagination begins to expand, as in a drawing of *Oberon and Titania reclining on a Lily*, afterwards used in the book called *The Song of Los*. But the drawing is still timid and without energy of outline.

In 1784, however, Blake produced a design,

slightly coloured, which already announces the maturing artist. This is *The Breach in a City*, in the Graham Robertson Collection, where, among bold broken shapes of masonry, by the strange light of dawn, women weep over their fallen dead and an old man on crutches looks down on his dead son. Here are the human forms which we are to meet again and again in Blake's work, not much different superficially from the forms we find in the art of the period but transfigured by an interior fire which gives intensity to attitude and gesture. It is a passionate design, such as no one else then living was capable of producing.

By profession an engraver, whose days were filled with laborious toil, Blake could give his evenings only to original work. Yet in a period of a few years, in the 1790's, he produced the most original of all his productions, the Illuminated Books, which are unique in the history of art, since he was the author of the text which he engraved and illuminated himself. Through his experiments with printing he was led to discover a new method of using water-colour. But indeed the copies of the *Songs of Innocence and of Experience* and the following Prophetic Books may be counted among the works of the water-colour school, since they are paintings, differing in colour with each copy, over a printed outline; and here the Indian-ink foundation is dispensed with. Through the recent gift by Miss Carey of her exquisite copy of *The Songs of Innocence and of Experience* the Print Room now possesses three copies of the book, in which Blake's variations of colouring may be studied. One of these books is made up from different copies, and a number of the pages are illuminated in opaque colour. How exactly the effect, which is sometimes of great beauty, was produced, it is difficult to say. But similar effects were produced in the great series of drawings made in 1795 by a combination of printing and painting. Blake had discovered that a millboard pressed down upon another board on which a design had been broadly laid in with oil colour left, when taken away, a granulated texture of pigment, deep and rich beyond anything that could be got by superimposed washes. And wishing perhaps to avoid the danger of flatness and emptiness in large-scale water-colours (for he had already abandoned the use of patterns on dresses and had no interest in the accidents of drapery), he employed this process for some works which in later years he was to equal but hardly to surpass. Incidentally the process enabled him to make more than one replica, for impressions taken from the original drawing could be worked up in water-colour by hand.

The series of colour-printed drawings includes the *Elijah in the Chariot of Fire, Hecate, Newton, Nebuchadnezzar, the Lazar House of Milton, the Elohim creating*

Adam, Satan Exulting over Eve, and *Pity.* Of some of these, two or three versions exist. *The Creation of Adam, the Elijah,* and *Pity* are pre-eminent among the drawings. Small as they are, compared with oil-paintings or frescoes of similar imaginative scope, they have an inherent greatness of conception which makes scale seem irrelevant.

For some reason or other Blake appears to have been dissatisfied with his experiments in opaque colour. For in his next undertaking, the immense series of drawings for Young's *Night Thoughts,* he returned to transparent tints. He made 537 water-colours, 43 of which were engraved by himself and published in 1797. For many years these drawings were for sale in London without a purchaser: they were then bought by the late Mr. W. A. White of Brooklyn, and his daughter, Mrs. Emerson, gener-ously presented them in 1929 to the British Museum.

Every hint of an image in Young's verse strikes a spark from Blake's brain, and immediately the large page, in which the printed text is inset, glows with a swiftly sketched design. The human types are in themselves conventional and sometimes absurd or grotesque, but they are acted on by a sort of whirl-wind force; limbs are incredibly elongated for the sake of expressiveness; the designs are always original, often splendid in their sense of irresistible movement. The water-colour washes are swept on with little care for evenness, the colours themselves simple and vivid. Though few of the drawings may rank with Blake's best, the cumulative effect of effervescent imagination and effortless invention in design impresses one with the feeling that here are pictorial ideas enough to furnish forth a whole generation of artists. Yet this immense series was produced after such an intense period of creativeness both poetic and pictorial, culminating in the grand drawings of 1795, as would have exhausted any other man.

The engraved *Night Thoughts* was a failure with the public. But fortunately Blake found a new friend in Thomas Butts, whose friendship and patronage enabled him to produce a steady stream of original works. He purchased drawings from Blake, sometimes at the rate of one a week, till his house was full of them.

For three years, 1800–3, Blake was at Felpham on the Sussex coast; the only years he passed out of London. He saw the sea for the first time; and the small but magnificent monochrome drawing, *The Spirit moved on the Face of the Waters*, dates from this time. Returning to London, he began to produce a number of water-colour designs, mostly illustrating the Old or the New Testament. These are unequal; but among them is the lovely *River of Life*, with its floating figures and ethereal colour. Another design of exceptional beauty is *The Angel rolling away the*

76

Stone from the Sepulchre in Mrs. Morse's collection. To the same period belong the *Famine* at Boston (1805), terrible in stark intensity, where the very tree rising against the desolate sky seems famished; and the *Fire* in the Graham Robertson collection, with its triumphant flames.

Milton also was illustrated in various sets of designs. A *Paradise Lost* set was made in 1807, and a new and superior set in the following year, now in the Boston Museum. *The Creation of Eve* is the finest of these designs. The designs to *Comus* probably preceded them. A series for *Paradise Regained* is un-dated. *L'Allegro* and *Il Penseroso* were illustrated about 1816. The designs for the *Ode on the Nativity* (1809) are in the Whitworth Institute. Few of the Milton illustrations rank with Blake's best work.

In 1809 Blake held a public exhibition of his works, confidently hoping for recognition. But it attracted few visitors and was a failure. The years that followed were years of poverty and neglect. But in 1818 Blake won a new friend, John Linnell, through whom he recovered his happy productive-ness and gathered round him a group of devoted disciples. To 1822 belongs Miss Carthew's *Wise and Foolish Virgins*, which equals the great series of 1795 and is one of Blake's finest designs.

Blake's last commission from Thomas Butts, who had bought continuously from him for so many years,

was a set of twenty-one designs for the Book of Job.
A little later, in 1823, a duplicate set was com-
missioned by Linnell, with a view to their being engraved. These illustrations to Job form the greatest
imaginative work of our water-colour school. It is
true that neither of the sets is quite equal to the engravings which represent Blake's final revision of the
designs; but the much larger scale of the drawings is
more fitting to their inherent grandeur, and in some
cases the fire and impetuosity of the water-colour
outweigh the superior felicity in design of the engraving. Both the Butts set and the Linnell set have
been allowed to go to America. In the Riches
(formerly Linnell) collection is a series of sketch
designs in pencil and wash on a reduced scale; and a
few years ago a fourth set of yet further reduced
drawings turned up in New Zealand and has also
gone to America. This last set is in water-colour
and of the same size as the engravings; it is very
interesting as representing a stage in the designs
between the Riches set and the final form which they
took on the copper. It is only in the engraving, for
instance, that the addition was made to the famous
design of *The Morning Stars*: the addition of the
lifted arms of unseen Seraphim at either side which
enhances so immensely its effect.

Blake's work in general is very unequal; but in his
Job we are impressed by the sustained power of the

WILLIAM BLAKE.   PITY

WILLIAM BLAKE.   THE WISE AND FOOLISH VIRGINS

whole series from beginning to end. One of the large-scale water-colours, *There were not found Women fair as the Daughters of Job* (No. 20), is a failure, because Blake had not thought out his conception; but the revised design, as it appears in the engraving, completely retrieves the failure. Apart from this, the series keeps a magnificent level of intense vision and dramatic force. The third illustration, where Satan brings destruction on Job's sons and daughters, is unequalled in energy and complexity: the eighth, where Job curses the day of his birth, in monumental eloquence of design and intensity of tragic emotion; the ninth, the *Vision of Eliphaz*, and the eleventh, *Job Affrighted*, in the expression of spiritual awe and terror; the twelfth, the *Speech of Elihu*, with its burning and dilated stars, holds us like a scene in a greatly acted play—but how can one choose? There are still *The Morning Stars*, and *God in the Whirlwind* and the grand serene conclusion. Blake, interpreting this ancient drama in his own sense, had found a perfectly congenial theme without having recourse to his own shadowy mythology: and he achieved (since the whole series must be regarded as one work) a masterpiece which holds one the more it is studied.

About 1824 Blake undertook a still more tremendous task, the illustration of Dante's *Divine Comedy*. This again was a commission from Linnell. Though now nearing seventy, he attacked the work with unflagging energy, and was occupied with it when he died. He made 68 drawings for the 'Hell', 20 for the 'Purgatory', and 10 for the 'Paradise'. Only a few are fully coloured: perhaps the finest of these is the *Whirlwind of Lovers* (Paolo and Francesca) now in the Birmingham Gallery. But I think the most beautiful drawing in the whole series is the *Pageant of the Church* in the Earthly Paradise, now in the Print Room; the drawing is in clear bright colours like the colours of sunrise, the river trembles with light, the ground is thick with many-coloured flowers. Very fine designs, less complete in colour, of Dante ascending the terraces of Purgatory, are in the Tate Gallery and at Oxford. The greater portion of the designs —many of them striking, but unequal— are in the Melbourne Gallery.

Perhaps because Blake was not a landscape painter, he has been ignored or dismissed with a line or two in books on English water-colours. This is absurd. In any sane view of the whole school such works as *Elijah*, the *Pity*, the *River of Life*, the *Wise and Foolish Virgins*, the *Job*, must rank among its chief masterpieces.

Blake was the one artist of his time who had intense imagination and the power to communicate it through line and colour. But in his own day I suppose that Fuseli enjoyed a similar reputation. There is one very large water-colour by Fuseli in the Print Room, *The Lapland Witch*, a single flying figure against a livid sky, which is probably his masterpiece; but his mind was shallow and theatrical, and very rarely is he so impressive. In fact what we now enjoy in Fuseli's work are his coloured drawings of seductive ladies dressed in a rather fantastic style; one or two examples are at South Kensington; there Fuseli, with his amorous temperament, is genuine; his heroics only amuse by being ridiculous. Thomas Stothard (1755–1834), on the other hand, falls on the side of insipidity when matched with Blake, who criticised his rival's picture of the *Canterbury Pilgrims* so severely. But Stothard had a graceful and abundant talent, shown to more advantage in his charming early illustrations to *Clarissa Harlowe*, which continue the tradition of Gravelot, than in his later water-colours. His collaboration with Turner in the illustration of Rogers' *Italy* is famous. By then his style had absorbed the facile grace of the Neo-Classic movement. There is much that is pleasant and pretty in his work, but it makes one crave for an astringent.

Another figure painter in water-colour of note is Francis Wheatley (1747–1801). Born and trained in London, he worked for a time in Dublin as a portrait painter, but returned to London and became R.A. in 1791. He painted largely in oils. At South Kensington the large *Meeting of the Dublin Volunteers on*

College Green (1779) is a very good example of his water-colours. Two illustrations to Rousseau's *Nouvelle Héloïse*, dated 1785 and 1786—figures in a setting of mountain and torrent—are more formal in style and seem to indicate a Continental influence. These are in the Print Room. In his *genre* subjects Wheatley is modish and pretty.

Richard Westall (1765–1836) worked chiefly in water-colours and was ambitious in style and subject. He painted historic scenes, rustics, and portraits, generally garish in colour, without the charm of liquid tints yet without success in manipulating the texture of heavier pigment. He is usually stagey and often ridiculous. His brother William was happier with his landscapes.

Though only a year or two younger than Richard Westall, Joshua Cristall seems to belong to a different generation. Trained as painter on china, he passed on to landscapes with idyllic figures from classic story, but found a more genuine vein in the painting of English rustic groups and scenes, free from the vapid elegance and sentiment of men like Westall and William Hamilton. Cristall was one of the foundation members of the 'Old' Water-Colour Society established in 1804, and was its president from 1821 to 1832. At South Kensington is one of his most 'important' works, *Fishermen on the Beach at Hastings*; and in such paintings, in spite of their merit, we see the prevailing ambition of the founders of the Water-Colour Society, which was to make their work look as solid and striking as oil paintings. Yet one cannot help feeling that oils would have been more appropriate to such efforts: in such elaboration the slighter medium loses its character of luminous freshness, the handling becomes tame and tired.

I find more pleasure in the village scenes of Robert Hills, better known for his drawings of deer and other animals, who was also a foundation member of the Society. In Mr. Girtin's collection is a drawing of a village in a snow shower, with rustics sheltering in a shed, which is intimate and homely and has real charm. Hills was born in 1769 and died in 1844.

7

VIII

GIRTIN

WITH Girtin we come to an assured strong
master, one of the greatest of English landscape painters, and one who, if we regard his relation at once to his predecessors and to his successors,
seems, even more than Turner in his dazzling isolation, the central figure of the whole water-colour
school.

Since I wrote my short study on Girtin in 1900,
the first monograph to be devoted to his work, a
good deal has been done, notably by Mr. Randall
Davies and Mr. C. F. Bell, to correct inaccurate
statements which had become current, and to clear
up obscure details in the artist's biography: some
new facts have thus been brought to life. Yet even
now there is much in the earlier part of his career
which remains doubtful.

Mr. Davies' volume, *Thomas Girtin's Water-Colours*
(The Studio, 1924), presents a fine array of paintings,
and is prefaced by a text which is notable for its scrupu-
lous care in setting out what is known for certain
and in sifting facts from the accumulation of legend.

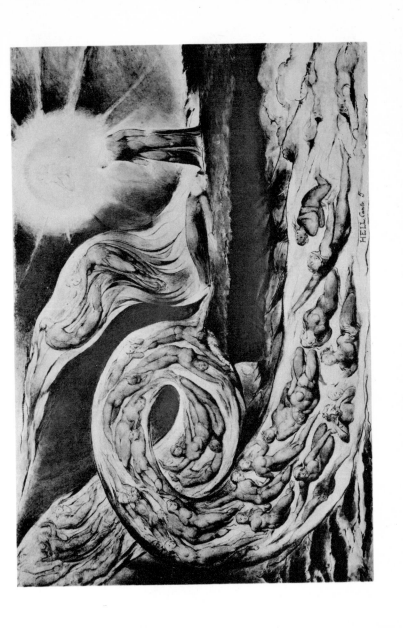

WILLIAM BLAKE.   THE WHIRLWIND OF LOVERS

THOMAS GIRTIN.   TYNEMOUTH

Thomas Girtin was born on 18th February 1775, in Great Bandy Leg Walk, Southwark. His father, a brushmaker, died when the boy, who was the second son, was only three years old. His mother removed to St. Martin's Le Grand. John, the elder son, was to become an engraver. Thomas showed at a very early age a passion for drawing; and after having lessons from a Mr. Fisher was apprenticed to Edward Dayes. Here uncertainty begins. The obituary notice in the *Gentleman's Magazine* merely says that 'he was, for a short time, the pupil of Mr. Dayes'. The natural inference is that he did not serve his full term as apprentice. And according to a much later story Dayes, jealous of his pupil's genius, set him to drudge at colouring prints, till the pupil, rebelling, was committed as a refractory apprentice to prison, whence the Earl of Essex rescued him by buying up his indentures. Recent research casts grave doubt on this story. What is the real truth about the relations between Girtin and his master we shall probably never know; we do know that, as Mr. Davies points out, he followed Dayes' style in his early years with extraordinary closeness; and in 1792 Dayes and Girtin were both working in intimate association with James Moore, Girtin's first patron.

After leaving Dayes, Girtin was employed by John Raphael Smith to colour prints. Smith was of a very different temperament from Dayes; he was a jovial member of the jovial circle in which Morland and Rowlandson lived; his drawings have an easy charm, and he was perhaps the finest of the fine mezzotinters who spread abroad the fame of Reynolds. Colouring prints was no facile task; it demanded a trained skill in the laying of even washes with the brush. And Girtin and Turner, who were now brought together for the first time in Raphael Smith's workshop, owed not a little to this training. The two boys were of the same age. They sometimes worked together side by side, as when they drew the ruins of the Savoy Palace. And being both at this time very much under the influence of Dayes, they produced drawings which it is often impossible to ascribe with confidence to the one or the other. Turner, taciturn and close, Girtin open and vivacious, they made a curious contrast in temperament.

James Moore, who was thirty in the year 1792, was a wholesale linen-draper in Cheapside, and lived in Southwark. His passion was Antiquity; and he travelled feverishly over the country in quest of subjects for his work, *Monastic Remains and Ancient Castles in England and Wales*, the first volume of which appeared in 1792. A consumptive, he died before the second volume was completed. His collection has only recently been dispersed, and a minute study of it has been published in the Walpole

Society's fifth volume by Mr. C. F. Bell, who secured
many of the drawings for the Ashmolean Museum.
Moore employed Girtin not only to make sketches,
but to make drawings from sketches of his own.
Girtin received six shillings for a whole day's work,
three shillings for a half-day. Through the material
in the Moore Collection, Mr. Bell has been able to
date Girtin's early drawings with approximate
precision.

The earliest of the drawings are connected with
Moore's tour in Scotland in 1792. Did Girtin accom-
pany him? The obituary notice says he did, and Mr.
Bell thinks it probable. Mr. Davies thinks on the
contrary that Girtin did not go to Scotland till 1796,
and that the Scottish subjects were worked up by
Girtin in London from sketches made by Moore.
However this be, there is no sign of the young artist
having been deeply affected by mountains and wild
scenery in these early works, as is suggested by the
obituary notice.

In 1794 Moore and Girtin were at Ely; and *Ely
Cathedral*, a drawing based on Moore's sketch, was
Girtin's first exhibited work, remarkable for a boy
of nineteen. In the same year he made two drawings
of *Peterborough* and *Lichfield West Fronts*, the first
works in which his genius begins to announce itself.
These were both in the Moore Collection. The *Peterborough* is now in the Ashmolean. In the Whitworth

Institute, Manchester, are rather later versions, interesting for the changes made in the design. In the original *Peterborough* the top of the near tower is visible; but in the later version it soars out of sight, with a far greater appeal to the imagination, and the Front fills the whole breadth of the drawing. In the *Lichfield* also the nearest spire reaches almost to the top of the paper, and the cathedral seems less removed from the eye. The sense both of towering height and of mass, especially in the *Peterborough*, is immensely enhanced. The great buildings seem to have dilated, to impose themselves on the mind. Probably the Whitworth drawings were made not long after the original ones, and they are a measure of Girtin's swift growth. For it is a real change that is denoted: we pass from drawings where the object before the eye is everything, and the artist sits apart from it, doing his best to represent it faithfully and effectively, to drawings in which it seems to assume a life of its own and to draw the artist to it, so that the result is a kind of fusion.

James Moore died in 1799, and after 1795 ceased to be associated with Girtin. But the brilliant young painter had attracted other friends and patrons. In 1795 Dr. Monro came to Farington seeking to get Girtin admitted to the Royal Academy Schools; and though nothing came of this, this new patron had an important influence on Girtin's life and art.

In 1798 Turner and Girtin told Farington that they had been employed by Dr. Monro three years to draw at his house in the evening. 'They went at 6 and stayed till ten. Girtin drew in outlines and Turner washed in the effects. They were chiefly employed in copying the outlines or unfinished drawings of Cozens, etc., etc., of which copies they made finished drawings. Dr. Monro allowed Turner 3s. 6d. each night. Girtin did not say what he had.'

Dr. Monro, as we have seen already, had Cozens in his charge as a patient from 1794 till his death (in or about 1799); and it seems plain from this statement that Monro, knowing that there was no hope of Cozens recovering his health, was anxious to complete the record of this favourite artist's work so far as it was possible to do so by this means. The employment of Girtin and Turner may well have begun in 1794. It was not, as used to be thought, in order to train the two young painters, but to add to his own collection that he employed them. Perhaps, as Mr. Oppé has suggested, he borrowed Cozens' drawings from other collectors for his purpose.

Dr. Monro lived in Adelphi Terrace, and another, younger, amateur draughtsman and collector, John Henderson, was a neighbour and employed both Girtin and Turner. All three appear to have made sketches together at Dover and in Kent in the summer of 1794.

On the same occasion in 1798, when Girtin and
Turner told Farington about their evenings at Dr.
Monro's, Girtin said that he had been on tour
through North Wales with a young man called Moss
from Norwich. 'Girtin had no money, so Moss ad-
vanced him £20.' Mr. Sydney Kitson suggests that
Farington misheard the name, and that 'Moss' was
really the painter P. S. Munn of *Greenwich*, who
was to tour with Cotman in 1801.

In 1796 Girtin came of age, and at the same time
entered into the full expansion of his powers. He was
in Scotland that year, as we know from a dated pencil
drawing of Jedburgh in the Print Room. It seems to
have been his farthest point north; and it was the
North of England, especially Yorkshire, rather than
Scotland, that impressed and inspired him.

From 1796 onwards we have no need to trouble
much about dates. Less than six years remained to
Girtin, but how full of creative energy! He had
completely emerged from his stage of pupilage to
Dayes, and looked for stimulus to quite other
masters. We are told that Canaletto first, and Rubens
later, deeply impressed him; but he had also learnt
what imaginative landscape could be from the drawings of Cozens which he had copied. There was then
of course no National Gallery; and young painters,
naturally seeking for great exemplars, could find
them only as fortune gave opportunity in private

collections. Girtin must have seen at Sir George Beaumont's the masterly *View of Venice* by Canaletto, now at Trafalgar Square, and probably some of that master's fine pictures of London. Mrs. Finberg's researches have shown that Canaletto was in England for about eight years, far longer than used to be supposed, and painted many pictures there. He was imitated by Samuel Scott and others, but his influence on Girtin was something much more truly fructifying and produced no superficial imitation. The broad pen-work of which Girtin came to be fond was probably an instrument he learnt to use so well from studying Canaletto's supple use of the reed in his sepia drawings. The broad planning too, and firm structure, of the Venetian's pictures must have attracted him.

In Rubens again he would have found abundant satisfaction of his own instincts in design; the wide prospects, the horizontal sweep, the confident attack on the main theme. But it is a case of discovered kinship, not of derivation. The mood is different, and in this respect indeed Girtin seems nearer akin to Richard Wilson or to J. R. Cozens, both of whom he had copied and studied. Yet here again there is a difference; and it is the difference more than the likeness which interests. Girtin is himself and no one else.

Much has been written about the transformation

of the water-colour school in the hands of Girtin and
Turner, as if it were chiefly a matter of technical in-
novation. As far as Girtin is concerned, the technical
change he introduced seems to have been the substitution of a warm for a cold underpainting. In spite
of contemporary statements, his palette was much
more limited than that of several of his predecessors.
And this restriction was no doubt of choice. For
emphasis on local colour tends to dissipate the strong
impress of a single emotional mood, which was
Girtin's aim. And it was the bringing of a new mind
and a new emotional power, no less than a superb
mastery of means, to the tradition he was bred in
that was the essential factor in the transformation he
effected.

In technical accomplishment Turner was, already
in 1795, the date of his *Lincoln Cathedral* and *Worcester Cathedral* in the Print Room, Girtin's superior,
at any rate in the drawing of architecture. They
differ in Girtin's preference for warm tones over
cold: but it seems to me that Girtin led the way in
emotional expressiveness; he is more direct, and con-
centrates more intently on his aim; sooner than
Turner he discovered the potency of the language
of light and darkness. Nothing is more characteristic
of Girtin than the wide sweeps of empty foreground,
leading the eye, unteased and untrammelled, into the
spaces beyond, where the main object of contempla-

THOMAS GIRTIN.   WHARFEDALE

THOMAS GIRTIN.   RICHMOND CASTLE, YORKSHIRE

tion is relieved and emphasised. The lesser men, and Turner himself, would be fearful of a foreground without 'interest'. There is a hint of this characteristic of Girtin's horizontal compositions as early as 1791, in one of his earliest known drawings, the *Rochester* in Mr. Coles' collection, which, as Mr. Davies suggests, seems to show the tendencies of the youthful artist when not working under Dayes' influence.

Girtin's methods can be seen from his unfinished drawings, such as the splendid *Cayne Waterfall* in the Print Room. The cartridge paper which he was the first to use has a warm tone, yet by a cunning opposition of blues this same paper, where it is left blank for the gleam of the falling water, appears pure white. The precision of the brush seems perfectly spontaneous, as it moulds the rocks and evokes the shapes or foliage and defines the interrupted threads of spray. Girtin's sureness of mastery might have been a danger to his art had it not been accompanied by an untarnished and deep sincerity and by continuous effort of the mind. We may feel at times that in the rendering of tree and foliage, for instance, he is contented with too easy a formula, yet we readily forgive him because of his concentration on the bigger things in landscape. At the present day, mastery of craft is often depreciated in favour of a sort of ferocious incompetence backed by good

93

intentions. But Girtin's mastery is a joy, because it is never mere accomplishment, never connotes (in Reynolds' phrase) 'mental laziness'.

Girtin loves his medium, and communicates his sensuous pleasure in the movement of his full brush over the sympathetic paper of his choice, leaving the rich blots of colour where he had placed them with so sure a touch. He had begun by drawing the subjects which his patrons demanded, old buildings and ruins, castles and abbeys and cathedrals. He continued to paint this kind of subject, but more and more we find him, as he expands and becomes more self-expressive, choosing his own themes. His horizons also expand. He paints Kirkstall in a large setting of ample moorland. He tends to see his landscapes from above, looking over wide prospects to the hills. He is animated by no vague romanticism; he sets himself to grasp and comprehend the structure of mountain forms; his art, masculine in its outlook, is enforced by knowledge as well as expressed with mastery of the brush. But he is romantic in his love of great spaces and solitude. He seems to breathe freest, to be most himself, where, as in the *Wharfedale* in Sir Hickman Bacon's collection, and even more intensely in *Plinlimmon*, in the Girtin Collection, he is face to face with the grandeur and solitariness of Nature. He was unlike Wordsworth in that he had an unfailing style at his command, but he was like Wordsworth—and both poet and painter were at their most inspired in the same years—in his native feeling for solitude and 'the sleep that is among the lonely hills'.

In the Print Room there is a series of small sketches, not more than a few inches in either dimension, which are worth study, for they show how instinctive was Girtin's gift for design. One is a sketch for the large *Stepping Stones on the Wharfe* in Mr. Girtin's collection: all the essentials of the perfected design are there, though in the large drawing the forms of the hill-sides are made solid, and the space is completely realised. Another is the little *Fields in Flood*—a fence across the flood, empty distance, waning light: it could hardly be more impressive if enlarged many times. There are some studies of sea and shipping among them; one is of three brigs sailing out from the land towards the spectator; two of the ships are in shadow, the one between, more distant, has sails of ghostly white. Girtin's eye is always alert for such pictorial motives. In yet another of these small studies, *Copenhagen House*, with its groups of holiday-makers strolling uphill to the house, all white under a dark sky, we find an anticipation of the motive of Girtin's most famous drawing, *The White House at Chelsea* (or *Chelsea Reach looking towards Battersea*, as it is more accurately described).

95

In this last drawing Girtin seems to throw far forward beyond his own time. It is dated 1800. Perfect in its poise, profoundly felt, this is a painting which we feel at once to be a classic. It is one of the loveliest of water-colours, one of the masterpieces of English landscape. It is not, it is true, typical of Girtin's main achievements, rather it points to the kind of landscape we should have had from him had he lived longer. More typical no doubt is the majestic *Bridgenorth* in the Print Room dated 1802, which is on a great scale, or the large and splendid *Knaresborough* (a distant view) at Manchester. Such paintings as these show Girtin's breadth and power more than the *White House*, but they are more imposing than intimate. Of Girtin's deepest feeling, indeed, they have less than the wonderful *Plinlimmon* in Mr. Girtin's collection, which is not a work to win the crowd, but is in its own way incomparable.

About the end of the century Girtin engaged on a greater undertaking than any he had hitherto attempted. This was a panorama of London, and is described as one of his only two works in oils, the other being the *Bolton Bridge*, exhibited at the Royal Academy in 1802. It is more probable that it was in distemper: that would be the usual medium for scene-painting, and this was a kind of scene-painting; and the drops of paint on one of the studies for the panorama show no oil-stains on the paper. Girtin painted two scenes for Covent Garden.

Mr. Finberg has unearthed and reprinted[1] an advertisement from *The Times* of 27th August 1802, which had escaped previous notice: 'Eidometropolis, a Great Panoramic Picture of London, Westminster, and Environs, now exhibiting at the Great Room, Spring Gardens, Admission 1s. T. Girtin returns his most grateful thanks to a generous Public for the encouragement given to his Exhibition, and as it has been conceived to be merely a Picture framed, he further begs leave to request of the Public to notice that it is Panoramic, and from its magnitude, which contains 1944 square feet, gives every object the appearance of being the size of nature. . . . His views of Paris, etched by himself, are in great forwardness and to be seen with the Picture as above.' The panorama was still on view in November, for on the 11th of that month there is again a notice to say that Girtin's exhibition will be shut till after his interment, when it will be reopened for the benefit of his widow and children, under the management of his brother, Mr. John Girtin.

What became of the panorama is not known. It is said to have been taken to Russia. Mr. Finberg's discovery is interesting because it makes us realise the

[1] 'The Development of British Landscape Painting in Water-Colours.' *The Studio*, 1917.

97

immensity of physical labour involved in such an undertaking, labour which may well have contributed to Girtin's untimely end.

Happily we have in the Print Room the studies for the panorama, which was semicircular. The view was from a point near the south end of Blackfriars Bridge, with the ruins of the Albion Mills, recently burnt down, in the foreground. One drawing is in pen and brown ink, recalling Canaletto in its easy mastery; the rest are in water-colours without pen-work, the brush-drawing firm and delicate at once.

In 1800 Girtin married and moved west from the artists' quarter in Central London to St. George's Row, Tyburn, where he had old Paul Sandby for neighbour. In the previous year was started a sketching club for the practice of imaginative or, as it was then called, Historic landscape; and though Girtin is not known to have been its founder he was by far its most distinguished member, and it came to be known as Girtin's Sketching Club. This is an indication of his maturer interests. To this late period belong some copies or adaptations of Canaletto, Piranesi, and Ricci.

But Girtin's life was already drawing to a close. His asthma was so bad that his friends were anxious and wished him to go to Madeira. Actually, he went no farther than Paris. He was there from November 1801 to May 1802. Though his health is said to have become worse, there is no sign of this in his work, which was more brilliant than ever. He made drawings of Paris, twenty of which were etched and published in aquatint; among them is the *Porte St. Denis* the drawing for which, without the figures, is in Sir Hickman Bacon's collection: another drawing of the Gate from a different point of view and in an even broader style, very massive in design, is at South Kensington. Both are reproduced in Mr. Davies' book.

It is to Mr. Randall Davies that we owe a very interesting discovery about some of Girtin's latest water-colours made in Paris; three drawings of great beauty, all signed and dated 'Girtin Paris 1801'. One is in the Victoria and Albert Museum, the other two in private hands. The first-named is an Italian landscape with a little town at some distance crowning the spur of a hill and a hermit and a crucifix in the foreground. Evidently a landscape which is imaginary or founded on a picture, since Girtin was never in Italy. And though the relation is not an obvious one at first sight, it is indisputable that here Girtin has taken an etching by Hermann Swanevelt, a Dutch disciple of Claude, and transformed it into this water-colour. The substitution of the hermit for the Holy Family and angels, a 'Repose in Egypt', is the least essential of the changes Girtin makes. He has removed a great tree from the foreground, simplified the main lines of the composition, given force and emphasis to what was dull and shapeless, breathed life and vigour into lifeless vegetation. I must refer the reader to the *Burlington Magazine* for May 1928, where Mr. Davies reproduces the three etchings with the paintings into which they have been transfigured. Anyone who wants to know what is meant by 'rhythm' in pictorial art should consider the difference between these two sets of designs, and see what it is which Girtin has and Swanevelt has not.

Born in 1776, Constable was one year younger than Girtin. It is recorded in Leslie's 'Life' that the whole current of his art was changed by the study of a set of thirty drawings by Girtin which he saw at Sir George Beaumont's. Girtin changed him, says Sir Charles Holmes, from an amateur into a painter.

In 1806 Constable visited the Lakes and made in that district a number of water-colours, now at South Kensington. He was strongly under Girtin's influence at the time, yet how different they are from Girtin's drawings of mountain scenes! Constable gives us the atmosphere of the hills, the 'wildness and wet'; but there is indefiniteness in the mountain forms, and little of Girtin's realisation of space: it is in their mood that the two artists are akin. These sketches of Borrowdale and Langdale impress one as the work of a sincere artist not wholly master yet of

JOHN CONSTABLE. STONEHENGE: THUNDERSTORM

J. M. W. TURNER. EASBY ABBEY, YORKSHIRE

his means of expression; we do not feel in them that congeniality of the artist with his subject that Girtin's drawings of mountain and moor immediately communicate. We know indeed that the solitude of the hills weighed on Constable's social nature; he was far more at home with the elms and rich pastures of his native county.

The water-colours of Constable's maturer time are very different from his sombre sketches made in the Lakes. They are fresh with green and glittering with light, or strong in contrast of storm-charged skies and gleaming earth. They are rarely anything but sketches. Constable's sketches are among his most brilliant work, but his oil-sketches are those in which his mastery is most apparent. Perhaps the most complete and striking of his water-colours is the *Stonehenge* at South Kensington, where rain and thunder are a congenial setting for the primeval stones.

Another great master of oil-painting who also, but less frequently than Constable, painted in water-colours is John Crome. Many water-colours ascribed to him are no doubt by his pupils, for he was a drawing-master in busy practice, or by other men of the Norwich School. His authentic works in this medium lack the skilled accomplishment of the professional water-colourists but have the same largeness of style that is in his canvases. In the Print Room there is a beautiful little drawing of a heath. *The*

Hollow Road, with its great white cloud, in the same collection, has the grandeur of conception of which Crome was always capable. But the finest of Crome's water-colours, so far as I know, is a drawing at South Kensington, curiously called *Landscape with Cottages*. It is a view up a lane, bordered by trees, with a glimpse of cottages on one side. It has a peculiar felicity in the laying of the colours on the paper, like that of Cotman in his early period; and the colour here is of extraordinary charm.

IX

TURNER

BORN in the same year as Girtin (1775), Turner also was a Londoner. His gift showed itself very early and was encouraged by his father, the barber of Maiden Lane, Covent Garden. When he was fourteen he was placed for a time with an architect called Hardwick, by whose advice he entered the Royal Academy Schools in 1789: landscape was not taught then, but he learnt to draw the figure. He learnt perspective from Thomas Malton, and coloured prints for J. R. Smith, at whose shop it is likely that he first met Girtin. Till about 1797 he and Girtin worked on parallel lines. They were a great deal together; and, as we have seen, for three years, probably 1794–97, frequented Dr. Monro's, and made a great number of copies after Cozens and other artists. Turner began to exhibit at the Royal Academy in 1790, four years earlier than Girtin, and was the better known of the two. He was soon busy in making topographical drawings, in which he seems to be more influenced by Dayes than anyone else.

The enormous mass of Turner drawings and

sketches belonging to the National Gallery, now transferred on loan to the Print Room of the British Museum, enable one to study Turner's work very fully, except for finished water-colours of his middle period, which are mostly in private hands. Mr. Finberg by his indefatigable labours—the official *Inventory* in two volumes, and the later commentary *Turner's Sketches and Drawings*—has put us all in his debt. These books are an indispensable guide to the vast collection in the Bequest.

There is a moment at which Turner's and Girtin's water-colours are practically indistinguishable. But before long the difference between them, as each develops, defines itself more clearly. Turner was gifted with a hand and eye of incomparable delicacy; he had an amazing visual memory, an inexhaustible appetite for observation of the subtlest kind. He was immensely ambitious, and his ambition was equalled by his patience and docility. By nature close and secretive, he was bent on learning and never ceased to learn, ready to take hints from any of the masters, while accumulating within his mind store upon store of first-hand knowledge through his eyesight. His sketch-books show how soon he acquired the power of drawing architecture with faultless ease and under-standing, if he does not give to the same degree as Cotman the sense of the roots a building has in the ground, and has little of Cotman's sense of pattern.

Wandering over England and Wales in the summer-time, Turner drew all the old buildings and ruins and famous prospects with his swift unerring pencil, choosing this subject and that for colouring in cool blues and greys. In 1793 he was drawing in Wales; in 1794 he made a tour through the Midlands. He worked for the engravers of the *Copper-Plate Magazine* and the *Pocket Magazine*; knew just what his public wanted, and supplied it. Good examples of this time are the *Tintern* at South Kensington and the large *Worcester Cathedral West Front* and *Lincoln Cathedral* (exhibited in 1795) in the Print Room. The *Lincoln* is rather prosaic, the *Worcester* more interesting with its tender evening light partly intercepted by the old buildings in the foreground.

In 1795 Turner made a tour in the Isle of Wight and South Wales: and in the sketch-books of this summer we find the artist breaking out from the topographer. Some at least of the drawings show him to be thinking of what pleases himself rather than his patrons. It is especially the sea which seems to exhilarate and excite him. Even as early as 1793, when, a boy of eighteen, he was at Dover making careful studies of boats in the harbour, the sight of a storm moves him to turn aside from routine and to make a sketch in colour, which, unfinished as it is, gives already a hint of the future painter of *Calais Pier*. From the South Wales sketch-book we see how intently he observes and tries to communicate the powerful movement of sea-water among rocks. There is in this sketch-book also a waterfall, identified by Mr. Finberg as Melincourt Fall, which renders very delicately the thin streams of falling spray, though the drawing is otherwise not to compare with Girtin's *Cayne Waterfall*. Moving water had already begun to fascinate Turner's mind. We note, however, that in the drawings of rocky streams which he made about this time the rocks themselves betray little of the sense of mass that Girtin gives. More than this, they are apt to be jumbled and accidental.

Turner indeed in these early years seems to be intent on accumulating facts of Nature which later he will draw upon to use and transform, whereas Girtin, even when sketching from Nature, seizes a pictorial motive which will be developed and emphasised in the finished work.

On the other hand, Turner is already more sensitive to the qualities of light. In the South Wales sketch-book there is an unfinished drawing of Maidstone Bridge, in which the vibration of the light is rendered with great delicacy. And in a water-colour of the year before (1794), *Warwick Castle*, with the river in front, Turner shows his originality of vision, and that peculiar caressing touch of his that seems to take the light itself upon his brush. A similar quality is in the *Pembroke Castle* of 1798; there is the same delicate tonality, the same cool colouring; it is a work of great charm.

Some excursions into a different kind of subject must be mentioned. The *Interior of a Cottage*, with children playing before the fire (about 1793), and another *Interior* with a woman bending over her pots and pans (about 1795), are less remarkable than the *Iron Foundry* of a year or so later than the last, where the molten mass of metal sends a glow among the rafters of the rude building. Evidently Turner was seeking to study effects of light and shade such as his routine subjects as a topographical draughtsman would not give him.

But he was soon to be studying light and dark in landscape with special intentness. In a sketch-book of 1795 is a water-colour of a windmill on a near hill, with a view into a valley below. It is a Girtin subject, but lacks Girtin's ease and breadth in contrasting tones. In 1797, however, Turner's powers expand remarkably. Girtin's Yorkshire drawings of the year before spurred him to emulation. In the summer of this year he went for a tour in Yorkshire, Durham, Cumberland, and other northern counties, and made sketches from which were painted the fine *Workworth*, at South Kensington, and the first version of *Norham Castle*. This last subject appears (though in a different composition) in the *Liber Studiorum* and in rich colour in *The Rivers of England*. Turner had noted the solemn effect of a mass of building thrown into strong shadow by the sunrise behind it. The *Norham* was his first great success. We may group with this the *Easby Abbey* in the Whitworth Institute, though it is a little later in date. This large and noble drawing rivals Girtin's masterpieces in the same kind.

Breadth and simplicity, shadow and light in massive opposition, seem to have had little natural appeal to Turner. But he could see how emotionally effective they were, and, determined never to neglect a resource, to have every arrow in his quiver, he used them in the *Norham* and the *Easby*. In the later finished water-colour of *Norham* (a different design) the deep blue of the tower and contrasted warm colours in the foreground detract from the felicity of the monochrome version in *Liber Studiorum*.

Already Turner had begun to paint ambitious pictures in oils, and Richard Wilson was the master he was especially studying. Such pictures as *Kilgarran Castle* and the *Dolbadarn* in the Diploma Gallery represent this phase. The effort to suppress detail results in a certain emptiness.

But Turner's native bent was not towards the reposeful grandeurs of broadly built design: it is the subtle play of light over diverse shapes and surfaces, the filtering of the sky into the earth, that attracts him and eagerly engages his eye and hand; the breaking of the light over accidents of ground

J. M. W. TURNER.　BARGES IN A SQUALL

J. M. W. TURNER   " BLUE RIGI "

and rising foliage, the losing of it in hollows where streams emerge and gleam; and this interest inevitably makes for multiplicity, though the larger lines of structure are always there.

In 1802, with the brief Peace of Amiens, the Continent was open after many years to English people; and they rushed across the Channel. Girtin was already in Paris, but before the year was out he was dead. Turner crossed to Calais—and the crossing gave birth to one of his greatest early masterpieces, *Calais Pier*—and travelled on to Switzerland. In the Turner Bequest is a large sketch-book, in which his first impressions of the Alps are recorded, just as they had been recorded by Cozens in 1776 and by Francis Towne in 1781. Turner has here parted altogether from the topographical methods of his youth. Instead of delicate washes on white paper, he uses body-colour for his lights on a thick grey paper which he scrapes and rubs for the more subtle modulations of tone. He is working, in fact, more like an oil-painter making studies for pictures, and he uses little colour; the majority of the sketches, indeed, have no colour. Where Cozens had seen the snow-shrouded mountains as ghostly presences, and Towne as naked symbols of Nature's terrors, Turner sets himself to seize all the complex structure of the Alpine scene, crag over crag, pine-fledged ridges, treeless heights, and the remoter summits throned above all in their white altitudes. Turner allows himself no facile emotion; he is most concerned, as usual, in amassing fact on fact and comprehending their continuous relations. But emotion plays its part too, one cannot doubt, when one looks at the impassioned sketches of the Mer de Glace and the heights and depths of the St. Gothard Pass. These drawings are sketches and studies only, but they are the sketches and studies of a great master. The Swiss drawings form a sort of interlude in Turner's water-colour practice.

In the previous year, 1801, he was working in Scotland, and in the Bequest are two beautiful sketches, *Loch Long, Morning,* and *Loch Long, Evening,* where, seizing the transient moment and having no time for elaboration of detail, Turner for once works with a swiftness and breadth like Girtin's but with an added luminousness of his own. How much more eloquent the medium is in such spontaneous usage than in the long series of water-colours, marvellous as they are in their own way, made for the engravers, to which we are soon to come!

Turner was now mainly occupied with oil-painting; it is the period of his great sea-pictures, and a little later of a group of pictures in serener, almost idyllic vein, which rank with his best work: *Somer Hill, Hulks on the Tamar, Walton Bridges.* But he had also ambitious schemes of furthering his fame by means of engraving. He had worked for the engravers in his youth; but now he was the master, not the servant, and was to train with exacting supervision a school of engravers to reproduce the qualities he wanted, just as Rubens and Reynolds had done before him.

First comes the *Liber Studiorum*, which, begun in 1807, was abandoned in 1819. The plan of the work shows Turner's comprehensive ambition in landscape. The whole visible world is to be his province. Most of the drawings, in sepia or brown wash, often enforced with the pen, are in the Turner Bequest. Being made solely as preparatory to the engravings, the drawings must not be judged as complete in themselves; some are dull, some are beautiful. Turner rarely uses his brown washes with the rich felicity of Claude in his sketches, though he excels in radiant distances like that of the *River seen from a Terrace* and the *Junction of Severn and Wye*, and in vaporous sunshine as in the *Raglan*. There are in the *Liber* a number of rustic subjects, men and women at work in the fields, which seem included more because Turner wanted to be comprehensive than from a natural bent towards such themes. They proceed from an intention of the mind rather than from an appeal to the eye. Turner had not the gift of discovering the beauty of natural action in the ways of men with the fruitful earth; here is no savour of the soil, no sunburnt homeliness. The plate called *Ploughing, Eton*, is almost absurd. It is not that there is false sentiment, prettifying, or theatricality; but Turner seems unable to be on terms of intimacy with the soil and those who live by it and labour on it through the slowly changing ritual of the seasons. And more than this, there is no savour of English country, of English character. How different it is with him when he deals with boats and waves! On his travels he was mistaken for the mate of a trading vessel.

Yet we note in the long series of elaborate water-colours of the middle period how fond he is of introducing figures, sometimes in crowds, into his landscapes. And this not, I think, merely to animate a foreground—they are usually clumsy and often distracting, but always occupied; it is rather because at this time Turner conceived his whole work in what one might call an epic mood. Like Wordsworth, he would desire that no painting should be considered singly, but all the varied mass of his production was to be contemplated as his interpretation of life and the world; and human beings and human doings were part of the landscape, with the rivers and the hills, and the woods, and the changeful sky.

This is the period of the numerous series of water-colours made for publication by means of engraving: the *Southern Coast*, 1814–26, the *Views in Sussex*,

The Rivers of Devon, 1815–23, *Richmondshire*, 1818–1823, *Rivers and Ports of England*, 1823–27, and the long series of the *England and Wales*, 1827–38.

These highly finished water-colours are represented in the Bequest only by the drawings for the *Rivers and Ports of England*, and by the beautiful *Ivy Bridge* made for the *Rivers of Devon*. Most of the *England and Wales* and other series of drawings are in private hands. But in 1910 the British Museum acquired through the Salting Bequest a small but fine and representative set, including *Richmond in Yorkshire*, *Louth* and *Lancaster Sands* (from *England and Wales*); *Weathercote Cave* and *Heysham* (*Richmondshire*); *Loch Fyne*, 1815; *Malham Cove*; *The Vale of Ashburnham* and *The Vale of Heathfield* (*Views in Sussex*); *Bolton Abbey*. At South Kensington are *Hornby Castle*, *Plymouth*, *Plymouth Hoe*, and *The Port of London*. But these and the *Rivers and Ports* in the Bequest are only a fraction of the great array of water-colours made for the engravings.

The impression left by these works (there are many I have not seen) is one of extraordinary power and variety. Yet, for me at least, there is no such thrill of pleasure to be got from them as from Cotman's Greta drawings. This is chiefly because of the peculiar use of the medium. As a rule—there are exceptions—they are so meticulously wrought that all immediate trace of the brush on the paper is submerged in a marvellous confection of colour; every device of wiping, rubbing, sponging, scraping has been used. The workmanship is subtle and complex to a degree. Effects of atmosphere and broken or trailing light are magically rendered; in the *Richmond*, for instance, where an impalpable mist of spray floats up in the sunlight from the river below. There are a thousand beauties of delicate detail to dwell upon, especially in the tones of blue. The sky is ever a potent factor in the design, and the manifold elements of the whole scene are cunningly united. Yet one cannot help thinking that there would be more pleasure for the eye if the drawings had been less wrought upon. And there is always such a quantity of secondary motives woven into the theme.

Though it is not of necessary value in a work of art, Turner's incomparable skill is a thing to wonder at; and we wonder the more when we realise, as Mr. Finberg has shown us, how some of the most elaborate of these drawings were made from the merest rudimentary note recorded many years before. Turner seems never to forget what he has once observed. But this method of reviving a scene from memory and shaping a composition out of what was a note of the facts is apt to destroy the spontaneity of the water-colour. And this loss is the more apparent in that Turner was prone to transform the

character of what he had seen, so that places like
Heysham and Dartmouth look like half-fanciful
Southern scenes, and have not gained by the transformation. Once again, as it seems to me, it is the
sea and coast that show Turner at his greatest. In
the three drawings of ports in *Rivers and Ports of
England*—*Portsmouth, Sheerness,* and *Dover*—there
is exuberant life, the animation of human effort
mingling with the buoyant motion of the waves; one
has the underlying sense also of Nelson's England; a
certain exaltation of feeling has gone into the artist's
brush. But far greater than these, fine as they are,
is the *Longships Lighthouse* (in Mr. Gerald Agnew's
collection); for in this magnificent water-colour
Turner is intimately himself; he is not taking up a
subject because it will fit into his scheme of publication; it is the elemental sea itself that dilates his
powers, and he paints it as no one else has ever
painted it; sea, lifted by storm till it seems to be part
of the smothered sky that crashes upon the obliter-
ated shore. Turner, as in many an oil-painting, has
painted it thus, with the screaming flight of gulls,
and spectral in a hollow of arching storm-cloud the
solitary lighthouse.

From this period, about 1817, dates a sketch-book
full of studies of skies, in which we find the rapid
notes from Nature which Turner used as a repertory;
slight notes in colour of transient effects which yet

give with extraordinary sureness a sense of the infinite depths of air, of the winds, and the diverse motions of the clouds, sometimes with enchanting colour.

In 1819 Turner went to Italy. In the Turner Bequest are sketch-books containing a number of water-colours, as well as pencil drawings, inspired by Rome and Tivoli, the Tiber and the Campagna, and Naples.

As usual, with his instinct to be always at work, Turner makes large comprehensive sketches, setting down in summary detail the complex assemblage of buildings and ruins, churches and bridges, without apparent thought of any special pictorial motive, but as material to be stored up in his marvellous memory. But there are some sketches which invite a more particular attention. One is the *Porch of St. Peter's,* where the architecture is sketched in with rapid mastery, but the interest is all in the shadow of a great arch glowing with reflected light. A note of black in a priest, and of colour in some children on the steps, relieves the paler tones. The motive is a pictorial one; but it was not the kind of subject for Turner's public; this was for his own pleasure. Still more remarkable, as showing the artist's tendency of mind at this period, are two sketches in some cathedral (said to be St. Peter's, though the arches appear to be Gothic) where nothing of form is noted in the high-soaring pillars, but only light, shadow, and colour.

We shall see the same preoccupation with the behaviour of light in interiors fully developed in the very remarkable series of sketches made at Petworth in 1830. There are sketches of room after room in Petworth House, with groups of inmates and guests talking, listening to music, standing about, resting on sofas; or just a bed with rose-pink curtains, or a dimly lighted sculpture-hall; but always it is the invasion of the light, and its reflections on contrasted surfaces and colours, that fastens Turner's attention. The Dutch masters had sensitively painted the diffusion of light in a room, on walls, tiled floors, furniture, and satin dresses; but with Turner it is the force, the exuberance, the action, of the sun-light, almost obliterating the figures and shapes it flows over, which is apprehended, as if he had divined what science reveals to us of its energy and power.

A second journey to Italy in 1828–29 had further stimulated Turner's growing passion for the glory of sunlight. Three hundred and ninety drawings grouped together by Mr. Finberg as ' Colour Beginnings' (Inventory, CCLXIII) are of great interest in this respect, showing Turner's later method of conceiving a design in colour as a foundation to the finished work. The transparent medium is spontaneously used, and a radiance is achieved such as had never been before attempted.

In the studies for the *Rivers of France*, however, as in the earlier *Meuse and Moselle* series, Turner uses a blue-grey paper and mingles body-colour with transparent tints and often considerable pen-work. He was able, I suppose, to get solid effects more easily and rapidly by this method—and the subjects were chosen with a view to the method—but the colour is often forced and unpleasant.

Many will feel, no doubt, that in landscape they prefer that an artist should discover beauty for himself rather than seek it in the obviously picturesque. These drawings were made with publication in view, and that perhaps influenced Turner's choice; but also he was attracted by the scenic; by views from a height over river and champaign, with cities on the banks and shipping on the streams. The courses of the great rivers of Europe, the teeming life of a continent, steeped in changeful splendours of sky, and the rivers animating it with their shining curves and themselves animated by the traffic they carry—all this appealed to his wide-ranging imagination. The sense of England which pervades the drawings of his youth and early manhood has expanded into a sense of Europe; but in the end this also merges into something wider and profounder, a sense of the whole related universe.

The *Rivers of France* drawings and those of the

Meuse and Moselle show that Turner was not less masterly in his use of body-colour than of the transparent medium: especially where stony masses like the fortresses of Luxembourg, Namur, and Ehrenbreitstein were main features of the design. Some of the drawings have magical effects of atmosphere. Yet we feel that his unique genius is not fully disengaged.

It is in the late, transparent water-colours of Switzerland and Venice that Turner releases at last his secret soul. There seems no longer to be any thought of a public; he is alone with himself. He still makes innumerable drawings, but in a different mood; it is no longer the accumulation of fact as material for later compositions, it is the immediate record of moments of intense emotion. The pencil-work is the briefest summary, or dispensed with altogether. In his earlier work, crammed with patient and subtle observation, it is the behaviour of light as it strikes upon infinitely varied impediments which absorbs his eye; now, it is light triumphant. Venice intoxicates him. With their floor of waters, reflecting every change of coloured air from dawn to sunset, buildings that seem hardly more substantial than their reflection intercept the beating of the light only to enhance its glory. Set between sky and sea, the city, partaking of both elements, melts and glows, trembles and flushes, like a living, palpitating thing. The elements, in their energy and radiance, mean more and more to Turner, the works of man less and less. At first sight it is the miracle of the colour, the luminousness, the indescribable delicacy, that holds one; but soon one marvels more at the amazing science behind it, the evocation of complex forms, however submerged in aerial hues, the fullness of the distances. It is the same with the Alpine scenes, where the mountains retain their sculptured form yet seem built of light and air; the lakes are unfathomable, the valleys recede into an infinite distance. The design is all in depth; whorls of curving cloud lead the eye on and on into a vibrating mystery of light, which unifies the whole fabric of earth and air and water. Never had painting communicated with such subtlety and power the sense of infinity. For it is not merely the sense of infinite recession that it gives, the attraction of a final peace, such as we find in the Umbrian painters; it is space conceived as something living, as a power which draws our spirits into itself but also wells out in impalpable radiance from the picture and absorbs and envelops our minds.

Later painters, like Brabazon, have tried to begin where Turner left off, but how flimsy appear their efforts compared with his! Renouncing, as it seems, all else in his adoration of Light, and Colour the child of Light, he retains unconsciously in an inexhaustible memory the surety of knowledge stored from a lifetime's unceasing observation. And just as we divine all that science behind the brief sketch of a transient moment, so in judging Turner's achievement it is the cumulative effect of his expanding power that tells, rather than a few chosen masterpieces. Incredibly copious, frequently unscrupulous as Shakespeare, with an eye on the public, whom in his heart he despised, he is no pattern of artistic integrity and often pays the penalty for the lack of it: yet his greatness stands unassailable. It is in its cosmic sense that Turner's art, as it finally unfolds his genius, surpasses all other landscape art of Europe.

X

COTMAN

WE must now go back to the beginning of the nineteenth century and see what other artists were doing. Girtin's influence, continued for some time after his death, was strong, and wholly beneficial in setting the standard of a broad and sober style. It affected, more or less, John and Cornelius Varley, Samuel Prout, Peter De Wint, David Cox, W. H. Hunt, Louis Francia; and as that influence waned, these painters became less broad and simple in manner, though no doubt winning more favour with the public in their several ways of development. Cotman, much greater than any of these, came to London as a boy of sixteen, just when Girtin was doing his finest work. He joined the Sketching Club and no doubt admired Girtin, but his own inborn vision was too personal for him to be deeply or permanently affected by his influence.

John Sell Cotman was born at Norwich on 16th May 1782. He was the son of a hair-dresser, but refused to enter his father's business and, in spite of opposition, determined to be an artist. In 1797 or

1798 he went to London to try his fortune. The painters with whom he mingled were draughtsmen bred in the water-colour tradition which was so largely based on topography: Cotman, coming from Norwich, had the simple dignity of Crome's earlier painting before his eyes; his outlook was more fresh and free. He was, besides, a born composer.

In the Print Room is an oblong water-colour, *A Backwater in a Park*, the motive of which is a fence and its reflections in water. Mr. Reeve, from whose collection it came, catalogued it with the date 'September 1798'. There is no date on the back of the drawing, and therefore good critics incline to place it later, especially as signed drawings of that year are said to be commonplace. But so precise a date must have come from somewhere, probably from an old mount, and I think that possibly after all, though I would not dogmatise on the point, it may be right: and, if so, it would point to an early phase when Crome's example prevailed, for the handling and the colour remind one of Crome, though with an added personal touch.

Certain it is, that after coming to London Cotman went through a phase which must be due to the influence of the London artists he was working with, especially that of Girtin. His natural bent was to make patterns out of dark and light tones, as we see in the monochrome drawings, made at the Sketching

Club, which survive; but in this new phase he attempted the chiaroscuro of Nature, subduing his colour, making little use of contrast, and avoiding sharp definitions of area. A fine example of this manner is the *St. Mary Redcliffe, Bristol,* in the Print Room, solemn in smoky twilight. Mood and method alike recall Girtin's *Bridgenorth* of 1802. There are in fact passages, where the surface has been wiped or rubbed to lighten a shadow and give texture, which are almost identical in the two drawings.

Mr. Sydney Kitson, in his essay in the 7th volume of the Old Water Colour Society's Club, even surmises that on his summer tour of 1800 Cotman was Girtin's companion: certainly both were in Wales that summer, and many of the subjects they drew were the same. The *St. Mary Redcliffe* may have been painted in 1801. (Two smaller versions exist; one in Mr. Girtin's collection.) In the following year, that of Girtin's absence in Paris and of his death, Cotman went to Wales again, with Paul Sandby Munn: and perhaps owing to the companionship and transient influence of this older but inferior artist, the lapse into naturalism is more apparent. Some water-colours of this episodic period would hardly be recognised as Cotman's by those unfamiliar with his career. He had at this time a trick of introducing reeds or rushes into his foregrounds.

In 1803 and the two following years Cotman

worked in Yorkshire. It is notable that, as with Girtin, and as with Turner, so it was with Cotman: Yorkshire had something inspiring in its scene that awoke the genius in each of them.

Cotman was fortunate in finding not only inspiring themes in Yorkshire, but friends of culture and intelligence to whom he became affectionately attached, and they to him. These were the family of Francis Cholmeley of Brandsby. The Cholmeleys were also friends of Mr. Morritt of Rokeby, who soon afterwards became intimate with Sir Walter Scott; and for six weeks in 1805 Cotman was Morritt's guest, though he paid a short visit during those weeks to Durham. He afterwards returned to Brandsby. This year he gave much of his time, as he wrote in a letter, to making 'close copies from Nature'. At Brandsby, he made numbers of pencil drawings of trees, now in the British Museum, remarkable for their grasp of the tree's growth and the attachment of bough to stem; it is this rather than the mass of foliage that absorbs his interest. And at Rokeby he made a series of water-colours on the banks of the Greta, which announce a new master unlike any of his predecessors. It is true that in some respects he resembles Francis Towne; like him, Cotman was nervous, febrile, sensitive to excess; like him, he combined the desire to seize the structure of things with an instinctive bent for pictorial pattern.

But in actual production their manner was widely different.

In these Greta drawings we may first note the artist's delight in, and respect for, his materials. Cotman at this time used a paper which seems to be of an ideal texture for his purposes; not hard enough or stout enough to withstand scrubbing and scraping, it is absorbent, and its acceptance of the stain of colour is a beauty in itself. And then we divine how different from the ways of the sketcher from Nature are the processes of this artist's mind, unconsciously working upon the scene presented to his eyes and controlling all its elements into a complex unity.

Yet pattern and simplification are never obtruded; on the contrary, so sensitive is the touch that it is the spirit of the place that seems evoked, clothed in its transient aspect and delightful to the senses. *Greta Woods*, in Mr. Lewis Fry's collection, is an upright drawing; a near view of a steep bank half covered with light foliage rising from the river; above, between more distant tree-stems is blue sky and a glimpse of white cloud showing through the arch of a half-seen bridge. The tender colour hovers between green and blue and grey, with contrasting glooms of hollow, or of shade upon the slabbed rocks emerging from the water that reflects them. So delicate is the foliage that it seems that at any moment it will lift on a breeze to make 'the soft eye-music of slow-waving boughs' that enchanted Wordsworth in a similar scene.

The same felicity of poise, lovely pattern, and truth to Nature, the sense of earth, of growing trees and stirring air, are in *Duncombe Park* in the Print Room, with its 'delicious solitude'. Also in the Print Room are the *Drop-Gate in Duncombe Park*, *The Scotchman's Stone*, and the now famous *Greta Bridge*. The *Drop-Gate* with its original motive of design, such as no other painter of the time would have conceived, shows Cotman's love of straight lines and sharp angles in contrast with the soft contours of flattened foliage. *Greta Bridge* is assuredly no 'close copy' of Nature; the chalk sketch for it (also in the Print Room), itself an adaptation rather than a direct study from Nature, shows with what sure instinct the rocks in the foreground have been redisposed. Yet even here there is no self-consciousness in the design, which appears as a gift of fortune: and we can taste the coolness of the air, the tranquillity of the gliding water, just as we follow with delight the almost magically sensitive delineation of the arch across the stream.

This sense of intimacy disappears in drawings like the *New Bridge*, *Durham* (Sir Hickman Bacon's collection), which has been recomposed in the studio, and is altogether more abstract in its bold suppressions and simplifications and design built up of contrasting areas of colour and sharp divisions; a very noble thing, but without the breathing bloom-like quality of the drawings just mentioned.

The *Durham* in the Print Room has majesty, and already shows Cotman as the consummate draughts-man of architecture. These Yorkshire and Durham drawings of 1805, especially those inspired by the Greta, seem conceived in a state of complete happi-ness; unlaboured mastery comes to the artist as if in a moment of illumination; hand and eye and brain and feeling are all in harmony. No lovelier water-colours were ever made.

For a few years Cotman's style retains this ex-quisite felicity of balance. At Norwich he draws a corner of the interior of the Cathedral (in the Print Room), his pencil delicately firm and unerring, the stains of colour delicious to the eye; and the outside of *St. Luke's Chapel* (in the Norwich Museum), grand in its delicate severity. And in quite different subjects such as the *Ploughed Field* at Leeds and *Norwich Market Place* we enjoy the same qualities. The former is reproduced in Mr. Oppé's valuable book *The Water-Colours of J. S. Cotman* (The Studio, 1923); the latter, remarkable for its sense of pattern, in spite of a crowded animated scene, is in the possession of Mr. and Mrs. Esmond Morse.

In 1806 Cotman had left London and returned to Norwich. What induced him to this step we do not know. Just as he was liable to acute dejection, so he was prone to build extravagant hopes on slight foundations. He appears to have thought that he could make a living by portraiture and have leisure for landscape at the same time. The fervent love of his affectionate nature for Norfolk and Norwich, and the formation of a Norwich Society of Artists, no doubt contributed to his decision. But it was undoubtedly a mistake; his expectations were delusory. One feels that if only Cotman could have worked in a centre where ideas freely circulated and in a responsive society, among emulous fellow-artists, his wonderful gifts would have found very different and far richer fruition. But the movement of the age, the impulse to naturalism, was all against his inborn genius; and if London was not a really propitious centre at this time, it could have given him more scope and more stimulus than Norwich. The thing he most dreaded was to become a mere drawing-master: but a drawing-master he was doomed to be, if much else besides.

In 1809 he married. This may be the date of the drawing called *Twickenham* (really *Cheyne Walk*, in the Colman Collection), unusually gay in spirit and delicious in colour. But from this year onwards his style begins to change; the colour becomes warmer and richer, his water-colours assume more the character of paintings and less of drawings. The *Draining Mill*,

Lincolnshire, and *Mousehold Heath*, both in the Print Room, typify this transitional manner.

From 1811 to 1823, when he returned to Norwich, Cotman lived at Yarmouth. Now begin his numerous sea-pieces, and scenes on the beach with boats on shore. Admirable as these often are, we feel that something has gone from Cotman's art, as if he were a little tired and subjugated by routine. The *Dismasted Brig* in the Print Room, with its subtle simplification and masterly sky, is one of the finest examples; and with that we may place the equally wonderful water-colour of *The Needles* in Mr. Colman's collection, reproduced by Mr. Kitson in the volume already referred to.

The three visits to Normandy, in 1817, 1818, and 1820—Cotman's only visits to the Continent—greatly stimulated him. He went to study and draw Norman architecture and made a very great number of architectural drawings, usually in pencil and sepia. The *Castle of Arques*, in the Print Room, drawn for the etching in his Normandy book, is a splendid example: one feels the foundations of the massive ruin deep in earth. But Cotman was also fascinated by the rocks of Normandy, of Domfront, and of Mortain; something in their hard angles, jutting ledges, and fantastic forms seemed to excite his sensibility in a peculiar way.

The Normandy sketches provided motives and

suggestions which were afterwards to be worked up
into many a water-colour. In the letters written on
these tours, which have been published by Mr.
Isherwood Kay in the Walpole Society's 14th and
15th volumes, there is a passage (dated Cherbourg,
1820) which shows the way in which Cotman at this
time looked at landscape (the italics are Cotman's
own): 'When sufficiently near to the Town you look
down upon it as upon a fine quarry of *dead silver* with
here and there a strip of gold and the light and
shadowed sides both coming off from *the deep azure
of the bay*, as one mass of rich and glowing *pearl
colour*'.

Cotman was now preoccupied with colour. While
his friend Dawson Turner found the climate of
Normandy not a bit different from that of England,
to him there was a glory and strangeness in its sunshine; and his memory strove to recall it in colour
after his return. But Cotman, unlike Turner, whose
mind was stored with subtle and unceasing observation of every change in light and atmosphere, could
not divest himself of his instinct for pattern and frank
contrast; and to evoke the glory he desired he became
apt to scheme his drawings in a strong opposition
of warm yellow and full blue. Sometimes he succeeds,
but much more often the result is unpleasant. It is
interesting to note that in certain early drawings—
there is one in the Whitworth Institute—Cotman

designed in a similar scheme of blue trees and yellow ochre ground, only in much lower tones.

Another type of water-colour becomes frequent in his later years. Mixing his pigment with sour paste, he was able to get a singular richness and luminous intensity into his colour, sometimes working almost entirely in blues, as in some drawings based on Cader Idris in Wales. Also now he finds a new beauty in the solemn foliage of trees. The very beautiful *Breaking the Clod* in the Print Room is in black-and-white and much earlier; the motive is now emphasised in the *Shadowed Stream* in the same collection. This is also a monochrome, though of warmer tone: but some of the late drawings of this kind are richly coloured; a beautiful example is *The Lake*, reproduced by Mr. Oppé.

Few, I think, would accord to these later water-colours the supreme place of the finest of the Greta series of his early time; but it was impossible that Cotman, with his impressionable nature, should stereotype a manner, however exquisite.

From 1824 till his death in 1842 Cotman was drawing-master at King's College, London; a post he gained through the warm championship of Turner.

Among the drawings of his later time are a number which have for subject places on the Continent which he had never visited. These are based on sketches by

J. S. COTMAN. ST. LUKE'S CHAPEL

J. S. COTMAN.   DROP-GATE, DUNCOMBE PARK

a friend, W. H. Harriott. They do not count in his achievement; and his experiments in romantic figure-compositions, if more interesting, are not successful. In his late period Cotman often returned to drawings of his youth, recomposing them with heightened colour. While his contemporaries were losing strength and style in a superficial kind of naturalism, he was formalising to excess and losing natural sap and savour. But at times he woke from his fatigue and dejection, notably in the last autumn of his life, when he went down to his beloved Norfolk and made a whole series of fine drawings.

Marvellously gifted by nature with a union of rarely combined qualities, Cotman was unstable and ill fitted to master the difficulties of a life depressed by incessant drudgery. Yet to the last he was an artist in all his fibres; he did not know how to be popular and commercial. He always retains, in Mr. Oppé's admirable words, 'his sense of the actual drawing or painting as a thing of artistic and emotional value in its colour, line and massing over and above, or, at best, through and through, the significance of the objects represented'.

Cotman's manner imposed itself upon other members of the Norwich school. His eldest son, Miles Edmund, caught his later style of drawing and colouring so dexterously that it is sometimes difficult to tell them apart. John Joseph, the younger, was more independent and made some remarkable drawings.

John Thirtle (1777–1839), when he remembered Cotman, could produce attractive and distinguished work like the *Boat passing under a Bridge* at South Kensington; when he forgot him, he relapsed into something like dullness. What Cotman gave was a certain squareness and stability of design; but none of the minor Norwich men was gifted by nature with his instinct for detail-suppressing simplicity and breadth. Thirtle's sketches are often delightful.

XI

DE WINT, COX, BONINGTON, AND OTHERS

FROM Turner and Cotman it is a descent to even the best of the other painters who flourished in the mid-nineteenth century.

Calling on Farington in 1801 the young Constable had complained that the painters who criticised him looked 'only to the surface and not to the mind'. 'The mechanism of painting is their delight. Execution is their chief aim.' Constable here laid his finger on a weakness which particularly beset the English school in the nineteenth century; and it applies as much to the water-colourists as to the oil-painters. Astonishing dexterity becomes quite common; but there are times when we are provoked to exclaim that the painter seems to have everything except a mind.

Some of the artists conspired together to found the Water-Colour Society in 1804, and exhibition began to be the final aim of the artist's work. To live, he had to please the public. The public liked to feel that the maximum amount of solid work had been put into what it bought; and so the painters were tempted more and more to bring their work to a tame laborious finish, to make their medium as nearly dumb as it could be. There was no lively current of ideas to stimulate and challenge. In spite of increasing prestige, the art of the water-colour was sinking into a decadence: I mean, a falling away from the true aim of art, substituting an external for an internal standard and the communication of facts for the communication of emotion. It is possible for work to be manly and breezy and yet fundamentally decadent.

This seems to me to be not unjust as regards the average work and the general tendency; but it is of course unjust to the better artists, though even Turner surrendered often enough to the demands and the taste of his public. Yet there are few of these artists by whom one cannot find drawings which show how very much more sensitive and spontaneous they could be when they chose to be themselves. For instance, the 'poetical' compositions of George Barret, reminding one in their drowsy unreality of a drop-scene in a provincial theatre, may make one feel that he is negligible; and then one comes across little studies of street or coast which are delicate and quite charming.

Again, in Mr. Oppé's collection is a drawing by John Varley (1778–1842) of the sun about to rise over a long line of the Welsh hills. It was obviously made for the artist's own pleasure, and that pleasure comes through to us. It has a sense of beauty rare with Varley, who began in a broad and sober style inspired by Girtin but, becoming a very successful drawing-master, acquired a manner adapted to his profession and produced a great number of pretty but rather lifeless compositions. In his earlier work, when he painted with his eye on the object, many pleasing drawings are to be found, though perhaps the water-colours of his less ambitious brother Cornelius (1781–1873) give us now more satisfaction. Cornelius was an experimenter in electricity, while John dabbled in astrology.

William Henry Hunt (1790–1864) was apprenticed to John Varley. His name is associated now chiefly with meticulously stippled still-life drawings of birds' nests, moss, grapes, plums, primroses, etc. But when young he made good, if not particularly distinguished, water-colours of London streets; later he painted figures and interiors, painted with extraordinary deftness of touch. When he painted to amuse himself and not for exhibition, he too could be charming. His portrait of James Holland at South Kensington has the qualities proper to a water-colour drawing: ease, lightness, spontaneity.

Copley Fielding (1787–1855) was another of Varley's pupils. He had little sense of design—that was the weakness of most of these painters—and was

often not even clever. His earlier drawings show some
observation; he had great manipulative dexterity
when he chose; but the great reputation he enjoyed
seems to have no foundation, though now and then
he rises above his ordinary level; and he had a sense
of space.

Another pupil of Varley's showed extraordinary
promise when young. This was William Turner,
known as 'Turner of Oxford', to distinguish him
from his famous namesake. At the age of nineteen—
he was born in 1789 and died in 1862—he produced
the *Wychwood Forest*, now at South Kensington, a
large, solid, and sombre painting in water-colour,
which, if somewhat heavy in the handling, is composed with a certain nobility of design; a serpentin-
ing tree gives a touch of shadowy menace; one feels
the awe of ancient forests. But this early work seems
to be his best. There are good drawings by him to
be found—I remember some of Stonehenge; but he
declined into a drawing-master at Oxford, contented
with his lot.

Peter De Wint at his best is so admirable a painter
that it is a little disappointing to find that he is not
greater than he is. He resembles Constable in his
integrity and directness, and his profound love of
the English country-side; he produced numbers of
delightful drawings, but never seems to have con-

centrated his powers on the production of a few absolute masterpieces. He ranks nevertheless among the major artists of the school.

De Wint's life may be told in a few lines. Born at Hanley in Staffordshire in 1784, he was the son of a doctor of Dutch origin, and showed a passion for drawing as a child. There was something Dutch perhaps in his stubborn, rather stolid, character. Refusing to pursue the study of medicine, he was apprenticed to John Raphael Smith, but released from the last years of his indentures on condition of producing eleven oil pictures; and he painted in oils, though the water-colour was to be his favourite medium. He became close friends with William Hilton, his fellow-apprentice, afterwards R.A.; went to stay with Hilton at Lincoln, and married his sister. The two friends settled in Broad Street, Golden Square, where Varley was a neighbour. De Wint became a teacher of drawing, and a very successful one: unlike Cotman, he was content with the drudgery which made his living, since at the end of every London season he could escape into the country and paint all day long. His painting time being the late summer and autumn, we find harvest scenes and woodlands in their first autumnal colouring among his most frequent subjects.

When young, De Wint resorted to Dr. Monro's for study of that collector's drawings, and the Girtins were his special favourites. We can well imagine this, when we look at such a noble early drawing as the *Westminster* at South Kensington, broad, simple, and luminous. De Wint's peculiar vein of colouring, with its preference for russet tones, was not yet developed. His was a nature capable of deep attachment to places. Lincoln, where he fell in love, was a place he delighted to revisit; not only the city itself, its cathedral, its old red walls and archways, but the surrounding wolds, the wide prospects over the fens, provided endless motives for his brush.

Wide prospects indeed, wherever they were, made a peculiar appeal to him, as to Philips de Koninck. He liked horizontal compositions, very wide in proportion to their height. He is said to have proposed to apply the principles of Dutch art to English landscape. If there is something akin to the Dutch masters in his work, it is an honest plainness of approach, a total avoidance of the ornamental and adventitious; perhaps also a fondness for the spaciousness of flat country; but no one could more intimately render the character of the English scene, and his animated brushwork is in the English mode. His figures of harvesters and countrymen belong to the fields; they are well drawn and well grouped, and are never mere picturesque adjuncts put in to enliven a foreground.

De Wint is especially associated with Lincoln and

J. S. COTMAN.   DISMASTED BRIG

PETER DE WINT. NEAR CHRISTCHURCH

the country round it. He had a great love of rivers, and was fond of Thames as well as of Trent. He preferred the North of England, but worked also in Devonshire, Somerset, and Norfolk. In some of his best drawings the sky is left blank, with a happy and reposeful effect.

De Wint is fully represented at the Victoria and Albert Museum. I have already mentioned the fine early *Westminster*, but there are many examples in that museum of his mature style, and the wide horizontal designs so characteristic of him. He is less fully represented at the British Museum, though the Print Room collection has been enriched of late years by examples from the Sale Bequest, and by one first-rate early water-colour from the Salting Collection. This last is a large drawing of a cluster of cottages and farm buildings with empty sloping ground before it and a pond where boys are playing. It is a plain, unprettified English scene, soberly coloured in russet and grey tones; but it is largely designed, the figures just in the right places; one is conscious less of the painter's skill than of the artist's mind. In much of De Wint's later work this serious power of design is weakened, though we can always enjoy his eloquent use of his medium.

David Cox was born in 1783; a year after Cotman, a year before De Wint. Like them, he was forced to become a drawing-master for a livelihood. He chafed under the necessity, but it was not till he was fifty-seven that he found himself able to break free. Some eighteen years were left him. His late works are his best.

Born in a suburb of Birmingham, the son of a smith, he was too fragile to follow his father's occupation; was apprenticed to a minature painter, who committed suicide, and then for some time painted theatrical scenery. In 1804 he set out for London, became a friend of Prout, and made small drawings for small prices. He had a few lessons from Varley, but otherwise was self-taught. He married in 1808, and lived for several years at Dulwich, drawing and teaching. In 1813 he became a member of the Society of Painters in Water-Colours. Towards the end of 1814 he took a post as drawing-master at Hereford. In the same year he published a *Treatise on Landscape Painting and Effect in Water-colours*. He had already published *A Series of Progressive Lessons* in 1811.

How different an atmosphere of mind these books show from Alexander Cozens' in the eighteenth century! It is the picturesque incident that pre-occupies Cox, not the larger relations of form or the relations of dark tones to light, or the principles of composition. He tells the student 'ever to keep in view the principal object which induced him to make the sketch'; from that the character of the picture

should be derived. And the kind of object which induced Cox to make his sketches was such as appealed
to the taste of the day; thatched cottages, ivied ruins,
old windmills, rustic bridges, dock-fringed pools,
stooping willows. The intellectual element is almost
absent from Cox's art, and the emotional element is
of the simplest. But he is very genuine in his simplicity.

In 1826 Cox visited Belgium and Holland, and in
the following year moved to London. In 1829 he
went to Paris, and there made some unusually fine
drawings. The *Church of St. Eustache* in Mr. C. E.
Hughes' collection is a very beautiful water-colour,
with a welcome touch of severity in it. It shows that
the painter had a sensitive mind, and could appreciate
architecture in other forms than the ready-made
picturesque. He paid a brief visit to the French coast
in 1832; but he was tenaciously English, and would
never go abroad again. The drawings of his middle
period, deft in touch and agreeable in colour, reflect
his delight in breeze and sunshine; but one is easily
satiated by the numberless hay-fields, distant castles
among woods, hilly blue distances, cattle-drovers and
peasant women, cottages, etc., which he produced
with such unfailing zest. I like much better his sea-
shore scenes, Rhyl Sands or Morecambe Bay, with
waves lively under a breeze, or wide sands animated
with little groups of people in the distance. These

keep their freshness. In their kind, they could not be bettered. And one is suprised sometimes by the force and breadth of a sketch which has style as well as swiftness.

In 1841 Cox gave up teaching and went to live at Harborne. Every year he went to Bettws-y-coed, and in the Welsh moors and valleys found matter for his best and strongest work. Lancaster and the Lune, Wharfedale and Bolton, were also favourite haunts. It is true that he never acquired a convincing sense of structure. There is a drawing in the Print Room of *The Strid on the Wharfe*; wild rocks through which the stream rushes, and thick woods on either side. The rocks have no shape, communicate no sense of resistance to the touch; the trees have no growth, give no sense of root in the ground; yet the bold brushwork gives an appearance of vigour. He is happier with rough moorland and blowing cloud. The 'Wildness and Wet' celebrated in Gerard Hopkins' poem were what he loved, and the passion with which he painted them lifts his art at its best from the rather commonplace picturesque, the rendering of superficial things, which forms the bulk of his work.

David Cox is richly represented in the British Museum, the Sale Bequest having added in recent years to the series bequeathed by Mr. Henderson a number of water-colours, including the very large

DAVID COX.   BEESTON CASTLE

R. P. BONINGTON.   PARIS: THE INSTITUT, SEEN FROM THE QUAIS

Beeston Castle with a stormy shower coming on, which is simply designed and has a certain grandeur. But no water-colour shows Cox to greater advantage than *The Challenge*, a wild bull on a rain-swept moor, in the Victoria and Albert Museum. There is an extensive collection of his work in the Gallery of his native city of Birmingham.

In the month before Girtin died, on 25th October 1802, there was born an artist who was destined to an equally brief career and to display a brilliance that won him greater fame. Richard Parkes Bonington was born near Nottingham, where his father, an exuberant hearty person, was governor of the county jail, till his radical talk caused his retirement; on which he took to art and married a school-mistress. In the winter of 1817–18 the family went to reside at Calais, a town connected by commerce with Nottingham. Louis Francia had just left England to return to his native place; he was then about forty-six. Noticing the young Bonington's aptitude, he took him as a pupil. The boy, after a short time at Dunkirk, went to Paris with a letter to Delacroix, then about twenty-one. Thales Fielding, brother of Copley Fielding, was living with Delacroix, who was much attracted by Bonington's handsome presence, quiet manners, and precocious mastery of the brush. His new friend's skill in water-colours, then 'an

English novelty' in France, was an additional interest, for Delacroix was working much in that medium.

In 1819 Bonington entered the studio of Baron Gros. This was the time when the pupils of David pelted Watteau's *Embarquement* with their dirty sponges, and the Neo-Classics had all the vogue. But Bonington's heart was with Watteau, and with Flemish and Dutch masters; he adored Walter Scott, and cared nothing for David and his Roman nudes. He loved to paint little water-colours, scenes from French history or from Shakespeare, such as may be seen now in the Wallace Collection: their deft arrangement of figures and attractive glow of colour were something new to the Parisians. Corot has recorded how one of these water-colours, seen in a shop-window, fascinated him and turned him from a loitering errand-boy into a painter.

At the end of 1820 Bonington was painting in Normandy; in 1823 he visited French Flanders. Scenes on the coast were his favourite themes, as they had been of his teacher Francia. Francia was a leading spirit in the formation of 'Girtin's Sketching Club'; and his early work is deeply influenced by Girtin, so that sometimes a drawing of his may be mistaken for the English master's. His finest water-colour, *Transports returning from Spain, 1809, in St. Helen's Roads*, now in the Print Room, follows Girtin in its breadth and sober tones. His later style is more commonplace.

Bonington's fine *Rouen*, in the Print Room (published as a lithograph), is rich in tone, but still somewhat sombre: he was before long to practise in the gayer tints and more sparkling manner of his matured style. Landscape painters are known by the kind of clouds they love. Bonington liked best a high white noonday sky, the thin fabric of cloud, broken here and there into blue, filling the whole scene with reflected light. Sometimes, to force the light into the gloom of a narrow street, he would introduce a splash of theatrical red. Such artifices remind us of Lawrence; and Bonington in landscape stands for the same tendencies of the time that Lawrence exemplifies in portraiture. Both were brilliant, but in both there is a love of glitter that betrays them at times into meretriciousness and disguises their more solid qualities. Before the *Sea-piece* and the *Piazza, Venice*, both oil-paintings, in the Wallace Gallery, or the *Jumièges* at Nottingham, we feel that Bonington ranks high. He is a born painter. And we can understand the pleasure that his water-colours, with their freshness, vivacity, and complete command of materials, gave his contemporaries. But the small figure-pieces of historical subjects, which once seemed so novel and welcome a change from David's Greeks and Romans, and indeed made Bonington a precursor of the Romantics of 1830, have lost that charm and now seem little more than costume-pieces. The landscapes have qualities more enduring; but even in them one feels that Bonington's extraordinary technical gift was also his enemy. There is none of the interest of struggle in his painting. Delacroix, who praised him so highly, noted truly his 'marvellous understanding of effect and the facility of his execution'. 'Effect' seduced him too often.

In 1825 Delacroix was in England, and Bonington met him there. Both went to study a famous collection of armour, fascinating to each of them. In the spring of the following year a French friend of Bonington's took him to Italy. They were unlucky; for it rained continually. Bonington was in a fever to reach Venice, the city of his dreams. He stayed there a month, working prodigiously. He returned by Bologna and Florence, and was back in Paris before June was over. In 1827 he visited London and saw Lawrence, whom he impressed. Again in 1828 he went to London, but by now consumption had got hold of him, and a few days after his arrival he was dead.

It is obviously impossible that Bonington in his short life could have produced more than a fraction of the paintings and drawings which have been attributed to him. Besides many copies and forgeries, the work of certain other artists whom he directly or indirectly influenced may be confused with his.

Thomas Shotter Boys (*b.* 1803, *d.* 1874) was actually a pupil of Bonington, who in Paris persuaded him to give up the graver for the brush, for Boys had been apprenticed to George Cooke. He became very well known through his lithographed work *Picturesque Architecture in Paris, Ghent, Antwerp, Rouen,* which appeared in 1839. A similar work, *Original Views of London as it is,* was published in 1843. Some of his water-colours were on a large scale, like the two views of Paris in the Print Room. Boys was an able draughtsman who caught Bonington's manner very successfully, but added little of his own.

Bonington founded a sort of tradition, which is seen in artists like James Holland and William Callow, whose work has at any rate liveliness as well as skill.

Holland was the son of a Burslem potter: he was born in 1800. He painted flowers in his youth, then turned to landscape, painting both in oils and water-colours. His sketches are sometimes delicately coloured, sometimes bold and vigorous; his elaborated work is less successful. He died in 1870. Callow was born in 1812 and lived till 1908. He too was an admirable sketcher.

More interesting is the rare work of J. Scarlett

Davis, who died young, at forty. He painted especially interiors of buildings, with figures, and communicates sometimes a sense of grandeur and ambient space which gives him a place somewhat apart among the water-colourists of his time. He uses his medium, too, with a felicitous lightness. Scarlett Davis worked for a time in France.

De Wint and Cox remained staunch in their love of English country; but early in the nineteenth century certain areas of the Continent were discovered and exploited as sketching grounds for English artists. These were those frequented by travelling English folk on their holidays; the nearer resorts, Normandy, Belgium, and the Rhine, supplied market-places with vast, gabled house-fronts and picturesquely costumed groups, castles on hills, churches; and water-colours of these were in demand as reminders of holidays abroad.

Samuel Prout was the most successful purveyor of these happy memories of ready-made romance. He was born in Devonshire in 1783, and began with coast-scenes, boats and hulks, often well composed, but in a rather heavy style, as if always conscious of the difficulties his perseverance was bent on overcoming. He had little natural facility and had bad health all his life. However, he learnt to draw architecture well, though never at all comparably with

Cotman; and certainly not better than Henry Edridge, whom he resembled in the style of his pencil-work. From 1820 Prout exhibited Continental subjects, beginning with Normandy. But while Cotman loved the Norman austerity, Prout's preference was for debased Gothic, the more florid the better; it was more 'picturesque'.

David Roberts went further afield, taking with him similar tastes. Born near Edinburgh in 1796, he began as apprentice to a house-painter, though interested in architecture from the first. Then he became a scene-painter for the theatre, and in 1822 began to work for Drury Lane with Clarkson Stanfield. Before long he was exhibiting pictures, and early in the 'thirties visited Normandy and then Spain, which provided him with many subjects. In 1838 he set out on a more ambitious journey, to Egypt and Palestine. His work is rarely interesting, but now and again surprises by something more than excellent workmanship.

Clarkson Stanfield (1793–1867) gave up scene-painting in 1829, but always kept something of the scenic style. He is perhaps best known by his sea-pieces. There is a small water-colour by him in the Print Room of an empty upland with a distant small town on the horizon dark under a rapid storm-cloud that advances to fill the sky. For such a drawing, felt as well as seen, one would give most of his finished work.

W. J. Müller produced a mass of work, both in oils and water-colours, before his early death in 1845 at the age of thirty-three. He was a painter of extraordinary skill, washing in a scene with broad and fluent brush, confident and accurate. His work can be well seen in the Print Room, where there is a series of the water-colours made in Lycia at the end of his life, as well as sketches from Egypt, and English scenes. His painting strikes most at first sight, when his great ability impresses: the more it is studied, the more it loses interest. Gifts of hand and eye are not enough in art. In fact, when one compares Müller's Lycian drawings with the same scenes as drawn by E. T. Daniell, also in the Print Room, one turns with relief from their external proficiency to Daniell's less accomplished but more sensitive art. Daniell was of Norwich, though not strictly of the Norwich School, a clergyman and an amateur and a friend of Turner. He has something of Turner's grasp of the main lines of a composition, and a feeling for space. These drawings are in pen, with some wash; but when he painted in pure water-colours there is the same sensitiveness.

J. F. Lewis (1805–76) is, like Müller, best known for his Eastern scenes. He had amazing ability both as a draughtsman and as a painter. Would he, in a different mental atmosphere, have risen to the stature that seems so well within his compass? Who can say? He has not as high a reputation as he deserves, for he was capable of exquisite things; he disappoints because he fails too often to transmute fact into idea, he too seldom seizes the truly pictorial motive. Yet his consummate technical gifts compel respect.

There are a number of other painters who might here be discussed, such as George Cattermole (1800–1868), with his pictures of romantic incident; Joseph Nash (1808–78), with his architectural interiors; the sea-painters George Chambers (1803–40) and Charles Bentley (1806–54); and J. D. Harding (1797–1863), so typical of his time: but as these, with all their accomplishment, are of no special significance, I shall pass them over and glance for a moment at one or two artists who were outside what might be called the main stream if it had not become a backwater, and who seem to me of more interest.

E. T. Daniell, of whom I have just written, is one of these: not having to make a living by his painting, he was not seduced by exhibitions and the public. Edward Lear (1812–88), famous for his Nonsense Verses, is another. He illustrated his own books of travel. There is a beautiful example of his watercolour at South Kensington, and a series of drawings in the British Museum.

More gifted and original than these is Richard Dadd, whose work was mostly produced in a madhouse. After travelling in the East he returned, to kill his father, the first on a list of people who he thought would be better dead, and being judged insane, he was confined for the rest of his life. He lived till 1887, and was born in 1819. Dadd painted groups of figures, highly romantic, or with some satirical intention. His drawings are full of personal flavour and admirable in their unforced use of the medium: but his most interesting work is imaginative; sometimes a scene from history or legend, sometimes, as in the *View of Port Stragglin* in the Print Room, a scene of pure fantasy; and these are wrought in a strange and exquisite technique of his own, marvellously delicate in colour.

There is also Ruskin, whose fantastic praise lavished on artists like Prout and J. D. Harding, while Cotman was totally ignored, seems now so astonishing. One is less astonished when one studies Ruskin's own drawings. Entirely analytic in mind, he was a most exquisite observer. His interest in geology drew him to observe and record the structure of mountains, but he seemed to have little interest in the structure of pictorial design: and he gave excessive praise, in the work of others, to drawing which communicated 'truth', that is, facts of Nature. His own drawings render details, whether of rocks or architecture, with delicate accuracy and a sensitive love of colour. The little view of Fribourg in the Print Room, a water-colour enforced with fine pen-work, has something of the quality of a drawing by Dürer.

XII

ROSSETTI AND THE PRE-RAPHAELITES

BY the middle of the nineteenth century the water-colour painting, exhibited in a gilt frame, was an English institution, and enjoyed high favour with the public. Conditions had changed, taste had changed, patrons had changed; all for the worse. The country contained immense wealth, masking immense misery. The aristocratic dilettanti, of the type of Sir George Beaumont, who collected drawings by Cozens and Girtin in portfolios, were gone; it was now the rich manufacturers who went round the exhibitions to choose something for their walls that would remind them of their holidays. It was a time of private extravagance and public meanness. The Cobden statue in Camden Town is a symbol of that epoch. Shabby streets, converging, fail to give any relief to what is a masterpiece of insignificance. In such a way did the wealthiest nation in the world do honour to its statesmen. All sense of public style was lost. In private an unutterable solidity was demanded for the furniture of the gas-lighted home. Without and within, it was hard for imaginative art to breathe.

It was in such an age that Dante Gabriel Rossetti grew up: and if we find fault with his imperfect achievement, we should never forget what a load he had to lift in attempting to renew the imaginative life in pictorial art. For it is not as if there were a strong native tradition to be revived. Rossetti, looking back, could find only Blake to support his own effort. And before we look at Rossetti's water-colours, let us glance back for a moment to a movement which stirred all too briefly in the little group of Blake's followers.

There is a tiny water-colour by Edward Calvert in the collection of Mr. Louis Davis. It is called *A Primitive City.* I do not suppose that Rossetti had ever seen this exquisite work, but it would have enchanted him, for it is far more akin to his own sensuous imagination than any of Blake's creations. It has the richly intimate vision of a medieval painting in a manuscript, yet it is no archaistic exercise but something intensely personal to the artist. There is a charm in every detail, and the spirit of the whole is truly poetic; it is serene and complete. The drawing was no doubt done at the same time (about 1827) as the marvellous little engravings on copper, wood, and stone, which make so astonishing an apparition at a time when Lawrence and Hoppner were the accepted idols, and are among the most precious things in the whole of English art. But Calvert did no more in this vein. The *Primitive City* is his one tiny masterpiece in water-colour. His comrade Samuel Palmer produced at the same time a number of sepia drawings, pastoral idylls, not so perfect as Calvert's prints, but of singular beauty. *The Bright Cloud*, of which there is a version in the Tate Gallery and a finer one in the British Museum, is the most complete creation among these drawings. Afterwards, while Calvert was painting his dreams of the early world in oils, Palmer elaborated his water-colours, taking to fiery sunsets in the manner of Linnell and toiling after rich effects, with far less felicity than he had shown in his few early water-colours, which have a feverish glow but do communicate his sense of the glory of the earth. It is strange that Calvert's most rare gift should have found so little fruition. But, as it is, he must not be forgotten as a precursor, though on a different path, of the Pre-Raphaelites.

Rossetti was born in 1828. His father was a Dante scholar, and he was steeped in Dante's poetry from boyhood. Dante's peculiar intensity of vision, sparing no significant detail, was, I think, what he set before himself, perhaps unconsciously, as his ideal in painting, at least in his early work. In 1849, when he was twenty-one, he went with Holman Hunt to Belgium and to Paris, and probably the delicately faithful glimpses of tree and meadow, and old walls and streams, on which the windows in Memling's pic-

157

tures look out, appeared to him the perfect kind of background for his own work. For what the Pre-Raphaelites revolted against was the 'generalised form' which Reynolds preached, just as Blake revolted from it in his day; the 'property' trees and scenic settings which both portrait and history painters used as long as the eighteenth century tradition lasted. Early Italian art they seem only to have known from Lasinio's engravings after the frescoes in the Campo Santo at Pisa.

Rossetti was to make a new kind of water-colour painting. Intensity of conception was his aim, the complete imagining of a scene; and to get the expressiveness he wanted he used pure contrasted tints, with the pigment as dry as possible, stippling blue on blue and green on green; a depth of impassioned colour. His method can be studied in the unfinished *Passover* in the Tate Gallery, where a fair number of his early water-colours are to be seen. We note, too, his love at this time of straight line and angle, such as the current tradition would have avoided. In the *Arthur's Tomb* over which Lancelot and Guinevere meet, to part, with what admirable force the white edge of the long shield at Lancelot's back and the white edges of Guinevere's dress slash into the colour-scheme! And in the *Wedding of St. George* there is the strong diagonal of the spear crossing the composition. In the *Borgia Family* at South Kensington on the other hand the whole group of figures are composed in a great curve, with a sense of movement into the foreground; a very original design, where formal and imaginative motive are fused. The *Mary Magdalen* at the Tate Gallery is again very originally conceived, though the strange colour, with the spotted green of the moss on the wall and stair contrasting with dull reds and purples, is not quite fortunate, if perhaps symbolic. Rossetti's colour is most potent where he works in a simple scheme, as in the *Mary Nazarene*, also in the Tate Gallery, or the *Salutation of Beatrice* in Mr. Cockerell's collection at Cambridge, schemed in intensities of greens and blues. A very lovely water-colour in the Ricketts and Shannon Collection is the woman's figure from the *Arabian Nights* called *Golden Water*; the same collection contains what is perhaps Rossetti's greatest design, the large pen-and-ink drawing of *Mary Magdalen at the Door of Simon. The Bower Garden*, reproduced in Mr. Radford's book on Rossetti—a maid bringing wine to her mistress in a garden—has the same rich simplicity and dignity as the *Golden Water*. At Oxford in the Ashmolean is the *Dante Drawing an Angel*, which shows Rossetti's power of dyeing a scene, with all its accessories, in his own imagination, and in which the figures are admirably grouped. But more typical of his peculiar genius is the *Fazio's Mistress*, which I know only from reproductions published long ago in the *Hobby Horse,* also in Mr. Marillier's book. The impassioned convergence of hands and faces round the face of the dying girl, the rich contrasted patterns of the dresses which yet seem no mere decoration but make an intensity of pattern, the play of dark and light tones, the completeness and unity of the design, proclaim this as a little masterpiece of romantic art. What a world away from the costume pieces of Bonington and lesser romanticists!

Rossetti's fame has suffered from the dispersion in private collections of his best, his early work, which is unique and incomparable in its kind. Take him, and his influence, away from nineteenth-century England, and what an immense impoverishment would appear!

Rossetti's ambition, as I said, was to re-create imaginative painting in England; it was only imaginative art which interested him; and instead of the convention in vogue, derived remotely, but so very remotely, from the grand Italian manner of the Renaissance, and prescribing heroic types, flowing drapery, vague backgrounds, studio lighting, the aim proposed was the intense imagining of a scene as it might have been in reality, men and women of individual character using the gestures of life itself, with living sunlight falling on grass and foliage that were green and not a shadowy brown. Delacroix had

RICHARD DADD.   VIEW OF PORT STRAGGLIN

DANTE GABRIEL ROSSETTI. MEETING OF DANTE AND BEATRICE IN PURGATORY

noticed and praised a tendency in the English school to turn from the Latin tradition and pursue aims more consonant with the Northern genius. Dante, with his eye always on the object, appealed to Rossetti as an exception from the grand Italian manner. Among the Northerns was Shakespeare, who alone had combined the creation of numberless real characters with grandeur of style and glorious poetry; and Keats, adored by the Pre-Raphaelites, had insisted on the virtue of 'distinctness'. These were poets, not painters, but what predecessors in painting could they turn to? Actually, of the painters before Raphael they knew almost nothing. And Rossetti was poet as well as painter.

Such an aim involved patient and intense study of Nature. To Rossetti this was only a means to the realisation of an imagined scene, and it soon wearied him. It was a strain; and that strain of tense effort makes itself felt in the imaginative work of the group, while it also gives it its virtue and fascination. The effort could not be kept up. The movement divided; the intense and detailed study was applied not to things imagined but to things seen; so that 'Pre-Raphaelite' became associated merely with a method of minute, vivid, literal painting, and according to Holman Hunt the essence of the movement was to paint 'the glory of the earth in actual sunlight'; while on the other hand Burne-Jones, whose great gift was

inventive design, returned to the studio and a clois-
tered atmosphere of dream, inheriting from Rossetti
only the passion for romance.

Millais, so gifted technically, found the oil
medium the more congenial. He made no such new
use of water-colours as did Rossetti. In the Whitworth
Institute there are some of the designs for the
Parables, well-known by the wood-engravings—and
they are among his very finest work—which are in
water-colour; and though in most of these the colour
seems rather an irrelevant addition, the drawing of
the *Foolish Virgins*, almost a monochrome, is of extraordinary beauty. With this we may place the
intimate little drawing called *Love* at South Kensington.

Madox Brown worked in water-colours as well as
oils, but with no intimate understanding of the
medium, such as Alfred Stevens showed in his rare
water-colour drawings. Whatever medium Stevens
touched, he was sure to use it with felicity, for its
special qualities and capacities. Louisa Lady Water-
ford had something of this felicity, though she
seemed unable to carry to completeness pictorial designs which were excellently conceived.

To return to the Pre-Raphaelites: Rossetti's first
version of his *Lucrezia Borgia*, afterwards to be entirely repainted by him, seems to have inspired
Burne-Jones to make the two marvellous little paint-

ings of *Clara* and *Sidonia von Bork* (illustrations to Meinhold's romance) in Mr. Graham Robertson's collection. I am not sure if these are actually in water-colour or in some sort of tempera; but Burne-Jones seemed to delight in making water-colours look like oils, and oils like water-colours: the story of the frame-maker who washed away one of his elaborate water-colours, thinking it an oil-painting, is well-known. He used pigment as dry as possible. Of his earlier work the *Merlin and Vivien* at South Kensington is a fine example, with its sombre glow of colour. His later manner can be studied in the *Flower Book* at the Print Room. Here, taking the names of flowers, or inventing them, he devises within a circular form romantic compositions which have great beauty and originality of design, though the figures are drawn from a rather languid memory. The colour is strange and rich. Though inspired by legend rather than by life, these inventions are truly pictorial.

Another artist of the group, Simeon Solomon, deserves a mention. He promised a real originality, in themes of a sort of ceremonial spirituality (if the expression may be allowed) combined with a deep feeling for sensuous beauty. But his life was disordered and his gift wasted.

XIII

REVIVAL

THE Pre-Raphaelite movement lost its first impetus very quickly: it dissolved; and there was little to disturb the general placidity of English art till the coming of the ideas associated with Impressionism. In 1875 death cut short at once the careers of three artists belonging to that group who by their designs for wood-engraving have made the Illustrators of the 'Sixties famous: A. Boyd Houghton, born in 1836; Fred Walker, born in 1840; and G. J. Pinwell, born in 1842. The pen drawings of these men were better than their water-colours, which are over-finished: in Walker's case, too, a thin, sweet sentiment is cloyingly felt in the colour and handling as well as in the subjects. Men who were much their seniors, like Frederick Tayler (1802–89) with his daintily coloured hawking scenes, and Sir John Gilbert (1817–97), that resourceful, robustious illustrator and master of crowded scenes, and Birket Foster (1825–99) with his trimly pretty corners of Surrey, continued to exhibit year by year with great acceptance and success.

DANTE GABRIEL ROSSETTI.   GOLDEN WATER

P. WILSON STEER.　SHADOWS

Albert Moore (1841–93) by his avoidance of 'subject', acquired a certain aesthetic prestige: his blonde girls on sofas in delicately coloured gowns declare their indolent curves to be innocent of thought or emotion.

In this period Randolph Caldecott (1846–86), reverting to a method akin to Rowlandson's, produced a number of delightful drawings which, being intended for engraving in colour, were content to remain drawings and not to rival paintings. Walter Crane also was doing his best work as an illustrator in colour.

But now the doctrines of Impressionism began to filter into England. The theory of Impressionism, that one should paint only the impression on the retina of the eye, was bound to be sterilising: the practice of those associated with the movement was better than their theories. Pigment was handled with more enjoyment, things were seen more freshly; for the moment it didn't seem to matter that design and structure were cast aside. There was a revolt against the stale confection of the popular water-colour, in favour of something that told of the painter's joy in simple vision; of something spontaneous, however slight in the fabric. The French impressionists were idolised: but so far as water-colours were concerned, there was no need to turn to France: it was merely a question of recovering the lightness, frankness, and freshness which delight us in the drawings of Gainsborough, of Constable, of Turner in his later years, just as they were now to do in the drawings of Wilson Steer. A. W. Rich indeed went back entirely to earlier English practice for his inspiration, especially to De Wint, though his style was his own. Steer and Rich exhibited at the New English Art Club, which had been founded in 1886, along with Henry Tonks and D. S. MacColl and Roger Fry; and these and others began to re-create the tradition of English water-colour.

Once again, as in the eighteenth century, it is the variety of personal style and use of the medium that interest. Charles Conder was painting on silk his visions of a voluptuous dreamland, in exquisite vaporous colour. This was something quite new in English art: but what could contrast more with such delicate evocations than Sargent's visual record of the dazzle of sunshine on Alpine valleys or Venetian canals, or Arthur Melville's pursuit of the violent effects of light in Spain and the East; a pursuit (so vain, after all) which some votaries of Impressionism found so all-absorbing? In Clausen's water-colours on the other hand a singular sensitiveness to light and atmosphere combined with a sure instinct for pictorial motive. Max Beerbohm, using the seduction of pale and tender tints to enhance the pungency of his satire; Ricketts, making his superb theatrical

166

designs vibrate with gem-like colour; among the landscapists, J. D. Innes, designing in a bold convention and with a half-fantastic vision of his own, C. J. Holmes, taking perhaps a hint from Hokusai's woodcuts for his vigorous simplification of mountain scenes, David Muirhead, the austerer Cameron, Muirhead Bone, Francis Dodd, Cecil Hunt; MacEvoy's elusive charm in the portraiture of youth, Philip Connard's brilliant landscapes with figures, Albert Rutherston's graceful use of line and tint—to name these, and others that one might cite, is enough to show what a profuse new flowering on the old stem of tradition had come to pass. But these, of whom many are happily still living and producing, are too near to us; their work will be appraised by future historians. I want merely to emphasise the diversity of gift, and the restoration to the medium of freshness and zest.

The recoil from Impressionism, in which all design seemed at last to be foundering, is less apparent perhaps in this medium than in the oil painting of the modern style. It might be thought that water-colour was unsuited to the new emphasis on solidity and stability, the hatred of all softness, the discarding of the effort to attain delicate truth of 'values' and that submission to Nature which absorbed the preceding generation. Again, there was no need to invoke Cézanne, for Cotman was there to show the way by his mastery of structural design. Sky, hills, and woods remain, but 'the picturesque' has changed its nature; the place of ruined castle and tumble-down cottage has been taken by steam-crane and gasometer. But liberation from the need to be faithful to surface and atmosphere has brought an increased responsiveness to the larger relations of form, and the water-colour, with or without pen or chalk, proves its capacity for a new expressiveness.

In landscape, the brothers Paul and John Nash, to name but two artists out of a number of gifted contemporaries, illustrate how in different but related ways a modern vision may be applied to that old native tradition, the course of which I have tried to sketch.

———

PAUL NASH was born in 1889, the son of a lawyer. He left St. Paul's school early to study art at the Chelsea Poly-technic and commercial art in Fleet Street: he afterwards attended the Slade School, 1910–11. He first exhibited, at the Carfax Gallery in 1912, work showing the influence of Blake and Calvert. After serving in the line in the 1914–18 war and being wounded, he was appointed a war artist in 1917. His war pictures exhibited in 1918 brought him im-mediate fame and showed his style definitely formed. His influence upon other artists was extended by his teaching at the Royal College of Art where he was Instructor in Design, 1924–5. Though his actual tenure was short his influence

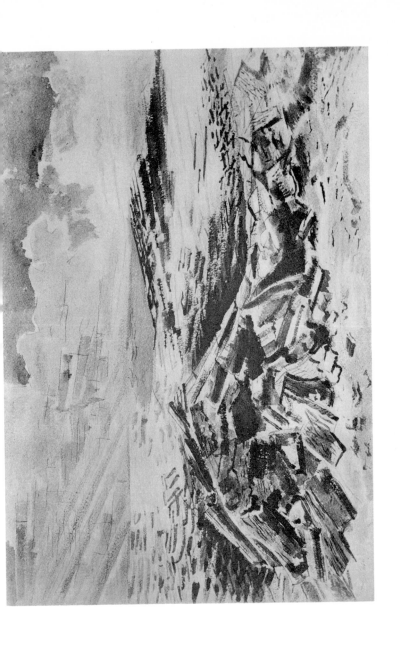

PAUL NASH.   WOOD SEA

DAVID JONES.　PETRA IM ROSENHAG

through this school has been profound. He has always been a painter in oils as well as in water-colours, often executing the same subjects in both mediums; but the number of his water-colours, the continuity of his work in this medium and his use of it as capable of finally expressing conceptions of importance, entitle him to consideration among the major artists treated of in this book. His vision has always been intellectual and imaginative, and more recently he has been connected with the surrealist movement. His ideas also have been influential; his writings include *Room and Book* (1932).

As a designer of patterned papers, book-bindings and textiles, and as a wood-engraver, he has been a pioneer in movements which are now transforming commercial art and book production.

EDWARD BAWDEN and ERIC RAVILIOUS, both born in 1903, studied at the Royal College of Art under Paul Nash, and have both themselves since taught there. They evolved, in the decade before the outbreak of war in 1939, a new method of painting in water-colours of great delicacy and definition, using a technique of under-painting and elaborate superimposed washes and stipples. Nearly all their paintings at this time were of the English countryside. As an official war artist Ravilious continued and developed his technique, executing particularly lovely paintings of sea and sky while he was with the Navy in Arctic waters during the Norwegian campaign. He was a distinguished wood-engraver, and did some colour lithography and designs for the decoration of pottery. He was killed on active service in 1942.

Since the war, during which he has travelled and worked in France, the Western Desert, the Sudan, Ethiopia, Palestine, Iraq and Iran, Edward Bawden's work in water-colours has developed, away from a rather tight and circumscribed style—not so delicate in feeling or in colour as that of Ravilious—to produce paintings with scale, body and romance.

Bawden has done publicity work for London Transport, Shell-Mex, the Curwen Press, etc., and been particularly successful in his designs for line-block reproduction. He has also designed lithographed wall-papers. In 1929–30 he and Ravilious executed mural paintings at Morley College, which unfortunately have since been destroyed by enemy action.

DAVID JONES, born in London in 1895, the son of a Welsh printer and lay-preacher, studied at the Camberwell School of Art (1910–14), and after the war, in which he served from 1915–18, at the Westminster Art School, 1919–21. Later he worked with Eric Gill. He has done important wood-engravings, some line-engraving and some paintings in oil, but the bulk of his work is in water-colours. Unlike the work of Paul Nash and his followers, his paintings are not predominantly landscapes but range, like those of Blake, though in less explicit symbolism, over the field of imaginative experience. His style, unlike theirs, is not structural, but pieced together from visual and symbolic scraps into a painfully wrought coherence. Since 1933 he has done little painting owing to ill-health, except for two Arthurian subjects which have been purchased by the Tate Gallery. He has latterly turned to writing as a means of expression. His book *In Parenthesis* was awarded the Hawthornden Prize for imaginative writing in 1938.

COLLECTING

I HAVE been asked to conclude this book with a few notes for the benefit of collectors. Though having myself no collector's instinct, I find it easy to sympathise with the collector; to feel the fascination of the hunt, at any rate, if not the joys of possession. And collecting is, no doubt, an education which can hardly be acquired in any other way; one is backing one's own judgment all the time. It is wonderful how much a training of the eye can do: most collectors must have experienced the astonishment one feels when confronted, after years, with something which once seemed so admirable and now seems so empty and poor.

The three things most necessary for making a good collection are knowledge, courage, and time. I have not mentioned money, because that is a relative affair, and a long purse is not so essential as one might think.

Speaking for myself, if I were a collector, I should collect the work of contemporary artists, especially the young. But human nature being what it is, one can understand why it is that so many prefer to buy the work of a past period: there is the enjoyment of the hunt, and the danger of being deceived, which adds such zest to that enjoyment.

It ought, no doubt, to be a matter of indifference whether a fine drawing is by one man or another. Quality, not authorship, is the thing that ought to count. All the same, the question of authorship does matter. For after all, the learning to distinguish a particular artist's hand from that of other artists, the master's hand from the good pupil's, is the best possible training that the eye and the judgment can have. Also, the personal element enters; you get to choose, your nature chooses for you, some particular artist or artists on whose work you look with a lover's eye. You may allow that, in an abstract comparison, the quality of some other painter is superior: but it is useless to reason, a scrap from the hand of your chosen one will be worth the most imposing work by that other.

English water-colours provide a large field for choice, and the production of the painters has been immense.

In the matter of prices, Turner stands alone. This is not only because of his fame, but because his slighter sketches are almost all in the Bequest and a national possession, while those which appear in sale-rooms from time to time are usually finished water-colour paintings and what are called 'important'

172

ERIC RAVILIOUS. CORPORAL STEDDIFORD'S MOBILE PIGEON LOFT

EDWARD BAWDEN.   GUBBA: PANORAMA OF THE TOWN

works. The elaborate examples of the other nine-teenth-century painters fetch less than they did, in some cases far less. Towards the end of the last century, an important David Cox could fetch £3000 or more. At that time a Cotman of corresponding rank would hardly fetch more than £30. But the prestige of the popular Victorian masters has waned, while the tendency is for the work of the earlier painters, headed by Cozens and Girtin, to go up in value; and the appreciation of Cotman has vastly increased. But, as I have pointed out in earlier pages of this book, one can often find slight works by the Victorians, done for their own pleasure, which give much more pleasure than their ambitious finished pieces. A collector of modest means should look out for these. Or he may prefer the sober charm of the earlier tinted drawings, unexciting but pleasant companions, which will also be within his reach. In any case he should follow his own instincts and buy what genuinely pleases him, and for no other reason. There is an unfortunate type of collector who rum-mage in small dealers' portfolios and in curiosity shops for drawings which they are determined shall represent some famous artist, however vaguely re-sembling him. They are always thinking of names, and they usually accumulate rubbish. They should remember that all unsigned drawings tend to gravi-tate toward celebrated names: and it should be their study to distinguish the master's hand from the follower's, a study which is the true collector's pleasure. We all make mistakes, and it is through mistakes we learn.

The first thing is to acquire a standard; and that means the study of really good examples. Happily, the public collections provide ample material. In London there are the two very rich collections of the Victoria and Albert Museum and the British Museum Print Room. The former is the better known, because there is always a large selection on exhibition at South Kensington; but the latter is equally rich, in some artists (Francis Towne, Girtin, Cotman, Cox) especially so; and the Turner Bequest, till lately in the National Gallery and the Tate Gallery, is now to be studied there. These two great collections complement each other. For Bonington there is the Wallace Gallery; and for modern water-colours the Tate Gallery, where there is also a small series of older works. Outside London, there is the Whitworth Institute at Manchester, a splendid and well-chosen collection; the Ashmolean Museum at Oxford; the Fitzwilliam at Cambridge; Leeds, Birmingham, Newcastle, Norwich (for the Norwich School); and other provincial galleries, generally specialising more or less on local artists of note.

There are also the sale-rooms. I mentioned time as an indispensable requisite for collecting. And if one has the time, assiduous attendance at sales, backed by comparative study in the public collections and courage in the judgment so formed, will still yield opportunity for acquiring fine work at small cost. As to the artists most worth seeking to have examples of, these pages have already indicated those who in my judgment are the best: but to each his own taste.

Of actual prices I will say nothing: price depends so much on circumstances that general statements can only be misleading; and I remember a saying of Charles Ricketts, a man of unrivalled genius for collecting: 'There is no such thing as a price'.

INDEX OF NAMES